CAPRIAL'S CAFE FAVORITES

Caprial Pence

TEN SPEED PRESS
Berkeley, California

TEN SPEED PRESS
P.O. Box 7123
Berkeley, CA 94707

Published in association with Culinary Arts Television

Cover design by Fifth Street Design
Text design by Linda Lane
Composition by Archetype Typography
Food styling and photographic conceptual development by Carolyn Schirmacher

Library of Congress Cataloging-in-Publication Data
Pence, Caprial.
          [Cafe favorites]
          Caprial's cafe favorites / Caprial Pence.
                    p.   cm.
          Includes index.
          ISBN 0-89815-600-9
                    1. Cookery.   I. Title.   II. Title: Cafe favorites.
TX714.P445   1994
641.5—dc20   94-13339
                                                                                      CIP

FIRST PRINTING 1994
Printed in the United States of America

6   7   8   9   10   —   99   98   97   96   95

To Savannah

another wonderful thing John and I whipped up!

ACKNOWLEDGEMENTS

To my husband, John, thank you for loving and supporting me in everything I do.

To the staff at the Bistro, thank you for keeping the restaurant going for two months without me!

To Merrillyn, thanks for the wonderful drawings and work at the Bistro during my absence.

To my parents, thank you just for always being there and always helping John and I to reach our goals.

To Chuck and all of the staff at the show, thank you for being patient and helping to make things run smoothly!

To Candace, thank you for all your work on the book—and to Carolyn and Ed. And to local potters Patrick Horsley and Stephen Gerould, thanks for supplying the platters and plates for the photos.

CONTENTS

■ Introduction *vii*

■ Appetizers *3*

■ Soups *23*

■ Sandwiches *35*

■ Salads *43*

■ Entrees *59*

■ Side Dishes *99*

■ Desserts *111*

■ Basics *137*

■ Glossary *147*

■ Index *148*

INTRODUCTION

My life is incredibly busy. My husband, John, and I run a small restaurant called the Westmoreland Bistro in Portland, Oregon. We have two little children. Here I sit, writing this book. And I've just finished shooting a television show for the Learning Channel. So, needless to say, I just don't have the time to prepare those elaborate dinners many people think we chefs sit down to when we're at home. But both John and I love good food and cooking, especially when it's for family and friends.

You're probably as busy as I am and as eager to share delicious meals with your loved ones—without having to spend hours in the kitchen. That's what inspired these recipes. They're meant to be user-friendly. And I hope that, even if you don't have a lot of experience, you'll find them easy to follow. People get so uptight about cooking, when it can be such a joy and a celebration. It's probably just lack of confidence. If this sounds like you, I hope that, with these recipes as your guide, you'll quickly discover that confidence. Soon you'll be creating wonderful dishes—everything from a potluck standby to a romantic entree for two. It's cooking for modern tastes, but never forgetting the best from our past.

I bring you the recipes for successful home cooking, but there are a couple of things you need to provide, too. First are the finest, sharpest knives you can afford. Now, I'm not saying you have to go out and buy $300's worth of knives. But know that it's more important to have a single good knife that a whole set of bad ones. If you're going to spend the money on just one, make it a good chef's knife. It will do a lot of jobs for you and last years and years. Have your knives professionally sharpened every once in a while and keep them honed with a steel. And never ever put your good knives in the dishwasher.

Next, you'll need quality pans to cook all these great dishes in. Again, you should use the best you can. If you don't already own one, I suggest you start with an ovenproof sauté pan that's about 10 inches (about 26 cm) in diameter. Then go on to the saucepans and other sauté pans.

Then, of course, you'll need the ingredients for the recipes. Always look for the freshest. Whether it's a single lettuce leaf or a fillet of salmon, learn which stores you can trust to supply you with the best. If you're in doubt, it's wiser to make something else. Because no matter how blunt your knives or scratched your pans, you can still create something wonderful if you have beautiful ingredients.

The last thing you need to be a great home cook is freedom. It comes with confidence and the knowledge that nothing is sacred. Feel free to change the recipes I've given you to create ones all your own. Substitute a little of this, add a little of that, and soon you'll have an exciting new dish. You can do it; I know you can! Also, give yourself the freedom to enjoy the process of cooking and sharing the pleasures of the table with others. Cooking is one of the few things that gives you such instant gratification. That feeling when you're hosting a party—or even just enjoying a family meal around the kitchen table—and realize that everyone is appreciating what you've just set down before them.

Now take this book and use it. Really use it. Splatter it with gooey stuff and bend the pages and make personal notes next to the recipes. If I came into your house, it would flatter me more to see my book a mess lying on the countertop than all pristine perched on a shelf. So enjoy yourself and share your joy with those around you. Celebrate life and all it has to give!

APPETIZERS

■ Chilled Shrimp with Smoked Onion Aïoli *3*

■ Herbed Baked Oysters *4*

■ Mushrooms Stuffed with Garlic Goat Cheese *5*

■ Sautéed Oysters with Tomato Pepper Relish *6*

■ Tomato Bruschetta *7*

■ Spinach Thyme Tart *8*

■ Herbed White Bean Spread *9*

■ Three-Cheese Quesadillas *10*

■ Spicy Cheese Puffs *11*

■ Vegetable Potstickers *12*

■ Brandied Chicken Liver Pâté *13*

■ Steamed Mussels with Basil *14*

■ Herb Custards *15*

■ Olive and Eggplant Tapenade *16*

■ Pan-Fried Oysters with Spicy Cabbage Salad *17*

■ Grilled Polenta with Roasted Tomato Sauce and Gorgonzola *18*

■ Sautéed Prawns with Sweet Peppers *19*

CHILLED SHRIMP WITH SMOKED ONION AÏOLI

SERVES SIX

The smoked onion in the aïoli lends this garlicky mayonnaise such a rich flavor. Dip a chilled shrimp into the aïoli and get a memorable meal of Chicken Breast with Apples and Gouda and Raspberry Port Ice Cream off to a great start.

24 shrimp (about 1½ pounds/750 g)
1 cup/250 mL/8 fl oz water
1 cup/250 mL/8 fl oz dry white wine
2 cloves garlic, coarsely chopped
3 sprigs fresh thyme, or ¼ teaspoon dried
1 lemon, halved

■ SMOKED ONION AÏOLI
1 teaspoon olive oil
1 small smoked onion (see note), coarsely chopped
2 cloves garlic, chopped
¼ cup/60 mL/2 fl oz white wine vinegar
2 egg yolks
1½ cups/375 mL/12 fl oz vegetable oil
1 tablespoon chopped fresh thyme, or ½ tablespoon dried
1 tablespoon cayenne or chile sauce
salt and freshly ground black pepper, to taste

Peel and devein the shrimp and set them aside.

In a medium saucepan over high temperature, heat the water, wine, garlic, thyme, and lemon halves just to a boil. Add the shrimp and cook until they turn pink, about 3 minutes. Remove the saucepan from the heat and set it aside to allow the shrimp cool down in the liquid. Place the saucepan in the refrigerator to chill the shrimp until ready to use.

For the Smoked Onion Aïoli, heat the olive oil until very hot in a sauté pan. Add the smoked onion and sauté for 2 minutes. In a food processor, coarsely chop the sautéed onion and the garlic. Add the vinegar and egg yolks and mix. With the motor running, slowly add the vegetable oil to blend thoroughly. Add the thyme and cayenne sauce and process until blended. Season with salt and pepper.

Serve the Chilled Shrimp with a dollop of Smoked Onion Aïoli on the side.

Note: If you don't own a smoker, smoke the onion on your barbecue over very low coals mixed with wood chips for about 1 hour.

HERBED BAKED OYSTERS

SERVES SIX

I've served these oysters to people who don't like oysters and made some converts. And if you do like oysters, you'll love them after you've tasted them with this crispy herb topping.

24 fresh oysters
¾ cup/45 g/1½ ounces bread crumbs
2 cloves garlic, chopped
1 teaspoon Dijon mustard
1 teaspoon olive oil
½ teaspoon chopped fresh thyme
½ teaspoon chopped fresh basil
¼ teaspoon chopped fresh marjoram
zest of 1 lemon
2 tablespoons grated Parmesan cheese

Shuck the oysters and set aside on the half-shell. Discard the remaining shells.

In a medium bowl, mix together thoroughly the bread crumbs, garlic, mustard, olive oil, thyme, basil, marjoram, lemon zest, and cheese.

Top each oyster with about 1 teaspoon of the breadcrumb mixture and place the oysters on a baking sheet. Cook under a high broiler (grill) for 5 to 7 minutes, or until the oysters are crispy and golden brown.

Serve the Herbed Baked Oysters hot, with a wedge of lemon and your favorite hot pepper sauce on the side.

Mushrooms Stuffed with Garlic Goat Cheese

SERVES FOUR

This appetizer followed by Beef Tenderloin with Three-Peppercorn Hollandaise and Chocolate Almond Cheesecake makes a very special dinner.

    20 medium mushrooms
    1 teaspoon olive oil
    2 shallots, chopped
    4 cloves garlic, finely chopped
    2 sundried tomatoes, chopped
    ½ cup/120 mL/4 fl oz dry sherry
    ½ teaspoon chopped fresh rosemary, or ¼ teaspoon dried
    1½ cups soft, mild goat cheese
    1 tablespoon unsalted butter
    salt and freshly ground black pepper, to taste

Remove the stems from the mushrooms and discard. Wipe the caps clean and set aside.

In a small sauté pan, heat the olive oil over medium heat. Add the shallots and garlic and sauté until they begin to give off their aroma, 2 or 3 minutes. Add the tomatoes and sherry, bring to a boil, and cook until almost all the sherry has evaporated, 4 or 5 minutes. Mix in the rosemary and remove from the heat. Set the mixture aside to cool.

Preheat the oven to 350° F/175° C/gas mark 4.

When the garlic mixture has cooled, add the goat cheese and mix together well. Stuff each mushroom cap with about 1 tablespoon of the garlic cheese.

In a baking dish large enough to hold all the mushrooms, heat the butter over medium heat. Place the stuffed mushrooms in the dish, cheese side up. Bake until the mushrooms are tender and the cheese bubbling, about 15 minutes.

Allow the mushrooms to rest for a minute or two before serving.

Sautéed Oysters with Tomato Pepper Relish

SERVES FOUR

Crispy sautéed oysters are a zesty start to any meal. I also enjoy them with Roasted Garlic and Tomato Soup for an elegant lunch.

■ TOMATO PEPPER RELISH

2 tomatoes, seeded and diced
1 red (Spanish) onion, julienned
2 red bell peppers (capsicums), roasted (see page 144) and julienned
1 yellow bell pepper (capsicum), roasted (see page 144) and julienned
3 cloves garlic, chopped
2 teaspoons grated fresh horseradish, or 3 teaspoons prepared
2 tablespoons red wine vinegar
6 tablespoons/95 mL/3 fl oz olive oil
½ teaspoon chopped cilantro (fresh coriander)
salt and freshly ground black pepper, to taste

20 small oysters
1 cup/155 g/5 ounces all-purpose (plain) flour
2 tablespoons olive oil
sprigs of cilantro (fresh coriander), for garnish

To prepare the Tomato Pepper Relish, mix together the tomatoes, onion, and red and yellow peppers in a medium bowl. Add the garlic and horseradish and mix well. Add the vinegar, 6 tablespoons/95 mL/3 fl oz olive oil, cilantro, salt, and pepper. Set aside.

Shuck the oysters and discard the liquor and shells. Dredge them in the flour. In a very large sauté pan over high temperature, heat the 2 tablespoons olive oil until smoking hot. Sauté the oysters, adding as many as will fit in the pan without crowding, for 2 minutes on each side, or until golden brown. Repeat with any remaining oysters, adding oil if necessary.

Place 5 sautéed oysters on each plate and top with about 3 or 4 tablespoons of the Tomato Pepper Relish.

Serve warm, garnished with a sprig or two of fresh cilantro.

Tomato Bruschetta

SERVES SIX

Only an Italian could transform a slice of toast into something so delicious! This garlicky tomato topping is my favorite, but Roasted Shallots are also very tasty. At the restaurant, many people like to turn this appetizer into a light lunch.

3 large tomatoes
4 cloves garlic, minced
6 cured black olives, minced
½ red (Spanish) onion, diced
¼ cup/60 mL/2 fl oz balsamic vinegar
⅓ cup/80 mL/3 fl oz olive oil
1 teaspoon chopped fresh basil, or ½ teaspoon dried
salt and freshly ground black pepper, to taste
6 large slices good-quality French bread

Cut the tomatoes into dice ¼ inch/0.5 cm. In a medium nonreactive bowl, combine the diced tomatoes, half the minced garlic, the olives, and onion and toss together well.

In a small bowl, combine the vinegar, olive oil, and basil. Add to the tomato mixture and toss together well. Season to taste with salt and pepper.

Toast the bread slices until golden brown. Spread with the remaining garlic. Spoon the tomato mixture onto the slices of toast and serve.

Spinach Thyme Tart

SERVES EIGHT TO TWELVE

A really versatile appetizer, this flavorful tart is also good for a light meal when it's paired with a green salad tossed with Sundried Tomato and Horseradish Dressing and crusty bread.

■ GARLIC CRUST

2 cups/315 g/10 ounces all-purpose (plain) flour
3 cloves garlic, minced
½ teaspoon salt
1 cup/250 g/8 ounces unsalted butter

■ FILLING

1 bunch spinach (English spinach, about ½ pound/250 g)
1 tablespoon/15 g/½ ounce unsalted butter
1 onion, finely chopped
2 cloves garlic, minced
2 shallots, minced
⅓ cup/80 mL/3 fl oz dry sherry
½ cup/90 g/3 oz good-quality Parmesan cheese
1 cup/250 mL/8 fl oz half-and-half (half milk, half cream)
2 eggs
1 tablespoon chopped fresh thyme, or ½ tablespoon dried
salt and freshly ground black pepper, to taste

Preheat the oven to 350° F/175° C/gas mark 4.

To make the crust, place the flour, garlic, and salt in a food processor. Turn the machine on and add the butter, 2 tablespoons/30 g/1 ounce at a time. Process until the dough forms a ball on top of the blades. Remove the dough and press into a well-greased 12-inch/30-cm tart pan with a removable bottom. Bake until the crust is light brown, about 15 minutes. Set aside to cool. Leave the oven on while you prepare the filling.

For the filling, wash the spinach and towel-dry it thoroughly. Chop it roughly and set aside.

In a large sauté pan over medium heat, melt the butter. Add the onion, garlic, and shallots. Sauté until they begin to give off their aroma, 2 or 3 minutes. Add the spinach and sauté just until it wilts, about 1 minute. Add the sherry and cook for another minute. Remove from the heat and set aside to cool.

Cover the bottom of the cooled crust with the Parmesan cheese. Add the cooled spinach mixture.

In a small bowl, whisk together the half-and-half, eggs, thyme, salt, and pepper. Pour into the crust over the spinach mixture. Bake until a tester inserted in the center comes out clean, about 25 minutes.

Serve the tart warm.

Herbed White Bean Spread

SERVES SIX

I like taking this to potluck parties. It always pleases vegetarians and non-vegetarians alike.

1½ cups/375 g/12 ounces Great Northern or cannellini beans, soaked overnight
1 small onion, finely chopped
1 carrot, finely chopped
1 stalk celery, finely chopped
3 cups/750 mL/24 fl oz Chicken or Vegetable Stock (see page 141)
1 head garlic, roasted (see page 144)
2 tablespoons chopped fresh thyme, or 1 tablespoon dried
½ cup/120 mL/4 fl oz olive oil
juice of 1 lemon
1 red bell pepper (capsicum), roasted (see page 144) and diced
salt and freshly ground black pepper, to taste

Drain and rinse the beans in a colander and place them in a large saucepan. Add the onion, carrot, celery, and stock. Bring to a boil over high heat, then simmer for up to 2 hours, or until the beans are very tender. Drain the beans and set them aside to cool.

Puree the beans in a food processor. Squeeze the pulp from the roasted garlic into the food processor. Add the thyme, oil, and lemon juice. Process the mixture until smooth.

Transfer the mixture to a large bowl and add the diced red pepper. Season with salt and pepper.

Serve the spread at room temperature, accompanied by toast and a selection of baby vegetables.

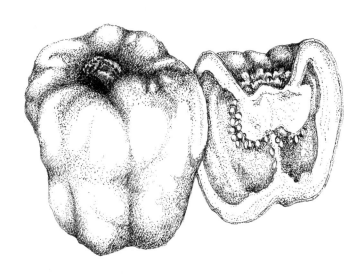

THREE-CHEESE QUESADILLAS

SERVES FOUR

Three-Cheese Quesadillas and Roasted Game Hens with Sweet Corn Salsa make an easy menu with spicy Southwestern style. If you're in the mood for dessert, add Cinnamon Rum Flan.

½ cup/90 g/3 ounces grated Cheddar cheese
½ cup/90 g/3 ounces grated Monterey jack (white mild melting) cheese
½ cup/90 g/3 ounces grated pepper jack cheese
8 large flour tortillas
½ cup/120 mL/4 fl oz sour cream (or crème fraîche)
½ cup/120 mL/4 fl oz Salsa (see page 142)

In a medium bowl, mix together the Cheddar, Monterey jack, and pepper jack cheeses.

Lay the 8 tortillas out on a cutting board. Divide the cheese equally among 4 of the tortillas, distributing it almost to the edges. Place one of the remaining tortillas on top of each to make 4 "sandwiches."

Place the tortillas on a well-oiled grill (barbecue) and cook for 1 or 2 minutes on each side, or until browned and crispy. Or place the tortillas under a hot broiler (grill) for 2 or 3 minutes per side.

Cut each tortilla into 8 triangles and serve warm, topped with sour cream and Salsa.

SPICY CHEESE PUFFS
SERVES FOUR

These are perfect holiday hors d'oeuvres or whenever you need a quick appetizer. Freeze a batch of uncooked puffs on a baking sheet, then transfer them to plastic freezer bags. Then you can just pop them into the oven shortly before your guests arrive and pop the cork on a bottle of brut champagne when they do!

1 cup/250 mL/8 fl oz water
½ cup/120 g/4 ounces unsalted butter
1 cup/155 g/5 ounces all-purpose (plain) flour
2 tablespoons cayenne or chile sauce
½ teaspoon cayenne powder
⅓ cup/60 g/2 ounces grated sharp cheese (such as Cheddar)
4 eggs
½ teaspoon salt
½ teaspoon coarsely ground black pepper

Preheat the oven to 425° F/210° C/gas mark 7.

In a medium saucepan over high temperature, heat the water and butter until they reach a rapid boil. Add the flour and stir until a soft dough is formed, 1 or 2 minutes. Turn the heat down very low and cook, stirring, for another 5 minutes to dry the dough out slightly.

Place the dough in an electric mixer. Using the paddle attachment, add the cayenne sauce and cayenne powder. Mix well, then fold in the cheese. Add the eggs one at a time, allowing each egg to be fully blended before adding the next. When all the eggs have been incorporated, the dough should be smooth and able to hold a peak.

Grease a baking sheet. Season the dough with the salt and coarse pepper, then place it in a pastry bag that has been fitted with a star tube. Pipe rosettes about ½ inch/1.5 cm diameter onto the baking sheet. Bake the rosettes for about 20 minutes. Turn the oven down to 300° F/150° C/gas mark 2 and cook for another 20 minutes, or until the puffs are golden brown.

Serve the Spicy Cheese Puffs hot.

Vegetable Potstickers
SERVES SIX

Here's another appetizer that's handy for the freezer. Freeze some of the uncooked potstickers on a baking sheet before transferring them to plastic bags, then steam them in the stock when you're ready. I like to serve them with Roast Duckling with Shiitake Fried Rice for an Asian-inspired dinner.

2 cloves garlic
1 teaspoon coarsely chopped fresh ginger
1 red bell pepper (capsicum), chopped
2 green (spring) onions, chopped
1 small carrot, coarsely chopped
6 snow (sugar) peas, chopped
3 tablespoons olive oil
½ tablespoon hoisin sauce or oyster sauce
1 teaspoon soy sauce
½ teaspoon sesame oil
1 package potsticker wrappers (about 40, available in Asian stores and some supermarkets)
¼ cup/60 mL/2 fl oz Vegetable or Chicken Stock (see page 141)

To make the vegetable stuffing, place the garlic, ginger, red pepper, green onions, carrot, and snow peas in a food processor. Pulse 4 or 5 times to form a coarse mixture.

In a medium sauté pan over high temperature, heat 1½ tablespoons of the olive oil until smoking hot. Add the vegetable mixture and sauté until the vegetables are tender, 1 or 2 minutes. Add the hoisin sauce, soy sauce, and sesame oil and sauté for 1 minute more. Remove the mixture from the pan and set aside to cool.

To prepare the potstickers, moisten the edge of a wrapper with water, using your finger. Place ½ teaspoon of the vegetable stuffing in the center of the wrapper. Fold the wrapper upwards upon itself to make little half-moon purses. Seal by crimping the edges together with your fingers. Proceed making potstickers in this manner until all the vegetable stuffing is used.

In a nonstick sauté pan over medium temperature, heat the remaining olive oil until very hot. Add as many stuffed potstickers as will fit in the pan without crowding and brown them on one side. Add some of the stock, cover, and steam for about 1 minute. Repeat for the remaining potstickers, pouring in more stock as needed.

Serve the Vegetable Potstickers warm, with soy sauce and Chinese mustard on the side.

BRANDIED CHICKEN LIVER PÂTÉ

SERVES SIX

Pâté can be both expensive and difficult to make, but this one is inexpensive and easy. Just make sure when pureeing the mixture that all the ingredients are very, very cold.

1 pound/500 g fresh chicken livers
1 tablespoon olive oil
3 cloves garlic, chopped
¼ cup/60 mL/2 fl oz brandy
8 shallots, roasted (see page 144)
¾ cup/180 g/6 ounces unsalted butter
¼ cup/60 mL/2 fl oz heavy cream
salt and freshly ground black pepper, to taste

Drain the chicken livers in a colander and set aside.

In a very large sauté pan over high temperature, heat the olive oil until smoking hot. Sear the livers on both sides. Add the garlic and brandy and cook over medium heat until half the brandy has evaporated, 2 or 3 minutes. Add the roasted shallots. Cool, then set the liver mixture aside in the refrigerator to chill.

In a food processor, puree the chilled liver mixture until smooth. Slowly add the butter, then the cream, and process until smooth. Season with salt and pepper and blend. Place the pâté in a container and refrigerate until well chilled.

Serve the Brandied Chicken Liver Pâté with French bread.

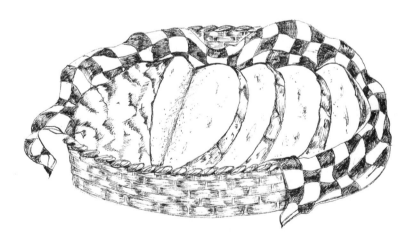

STEAMED MUSSELS WITH BASIL

SERVES FOUR

Treat your guests to the flavors of the Far East and accompany these aromatic mussels with Flank Steak with Asian Barbecue Sauce and Plum Spice Cake at your next summer dinner party.

4 pounds fresh mussels
3 shallots, chopped
3 cloves garlic
1 tablespoon chopped fresh ginger
½ cup/120 mL/4 fl oz mirin wine or sweet cooking wine
½ cup/120 mL/4 fl oz coconut milk
juice of 1 lime
2 tablespoons chopped fresh basil, or 1 tablespoon dried
salt and freshly ground black pepper, to taste
chile oil, to taste (optional)

Debeard the mussels and scrub them well. Set aside.

In a very large stockpot over high temperature, heat the shallots, garlic, ginger, wine, coconut milk, lime juice, and basil just to a boil. Add the mussels. Cover and cook for 7 to 10 minutes, or until all the mussels have opened. Discard any that have not opened after 10 minutes.

Remove the mussels from the pan with a slotted spoon and distribute them among 4 bowls. Season the broth with salt and pepper to taste, adding chile oil if you prefer a spicier taste.

Pour the broth over the mussels and serve hot.

HERB CUSTARDS

SERVES SIX

These custards are wonderful either as an appetizer or for brunch when they're paired with Caramelized-Onion and Potato Gratin and Ricotta Raspberry Tart.

2 teaspoons chopped fresh herbs (such as basil, thyme, rosemary)
4 eggs
3 cups/750 mL/24 fl oz half-and-half (half milk, half cream)
6 shallots, roasted (see page 144) and chopped
2 cloves garlic, chopped
¼ cup/45 g/1½ ounces grated Parmesan cheese
½ teaspoon salt
½ teaspoon freshly ground black pepper

Preheat the oven to 350° F/175° C/gas mark 4.

Finely chop the chosen herbs. In a large bowl, mix together well the eggs and half-and-half. Add the shallots, garlic, and cheese and mix thoroughly. Season with salt and pepper.

Pour the mixture into 6 custard cups (about 8 fl oz/250 mL). Place the cups in a deep baking dish and pour enough warm water into the dish to come halfway up the sides of the cups. Bake for 40 to 50 minutes, or until a tester inserted in the center of the custard comes out clean.

Serve warm or cold.

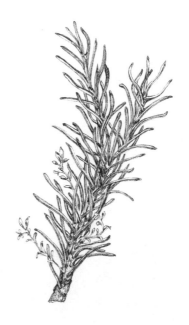

OLIVE AND EGGPLANT TAPENADE

SERVES SIX

Don't just serve this simple garlicky spread as an appetizer. It's also delicious dolloped on top of some rare grilled ahi tuna or tossed with pasta.

1 large eggplant (aubergine)
¼ cup/60 mL/2 fl oz plus 1 teaspoon olive oil
1 cup/90 g/3 ounces Kalamata olives, pitted
2 anchovy fillets
1 teaspoon capers
4 cloves garlic
freshly ground black pepper, to taste

Preheat the oven to 425° F/210° C/gas mark 7.

Coat the eggplant with 1 teaspoon of the olive oil. Place the eggplant on a baking sheet and roast it for about 20 minutes, or until the skin is blistered and brown. Set aside and peel when cool enough to handle.

Place the eggplant, olives, anchovies, capers, and garlic in a food processor and blend. Once the mixture is pureed, drizzle in the remaining olive oil. Process until the mixture resembles a rough paste.

Serve Olive and Eggplant Tapenade at room temperature with crackers, pita bread, or French bread.

PAN-FRIED OYSTERS
WITH SPICY CABBAGE SALAD

SERVES FOUR

We've served this dish at our restaurant for years and I'm not sure our customers will ever let us take it off the menu. I hope it becomes as loved in your kitchen.

■ SPICY CABBAGE SALAD
4 cups/1 kg/34 ounces thinly sliced red cabbage (1 medium cabbage)
2 cloves garlic
1 tablespoon chopped fresh ginger
¼ cup/60 mL/2 fl oz (clear) honey
juice of 1 lemon
juice of 1 lime
1 tablespoon chile paste
2 teaspoons sesame oil
¼ cup/60 mL/2 fl oz vegetable oil
salt and freshly ground black pepper, to taste

1 cup/155 g/5 ounces all-purpose (plain) flour
1 teaspoon fresh thyme, or ½ teaspoon dried
1 teaspoon fresh basil, or ½ teaspoon dried
1 teaspoon freshly ground black pepper
1 teaspoon salt
2 tablespoons olive oil
20 small fresh oysters, shucked

To make the salad, place the cabbage in a medium nonreactive bowl and set aside.

In a small bowl, whisk together the garlic, ginger, honey, lemon juice, lime juice, and chile paste. Whisk in the sesame oil slowly to blend thoroughly. Then whisk in the vegetable oil slowly and blend thoroughly. Season to taste with salt and pepper.

Pour the oil mixture over the cabbage and toss to combine. Set aside for at least 30 minutes to allow the flavors to develop, and then divide among 4 salad plates.

In another small bowl, mix together the flour, thyme, basil, pepper, and salt.

In a large sauté pan over high temperature, heat the olive oil until very hot. Dredge the oysters in the seasoned flour. Add as many oysters as will fit in the pan without crowding and sauté until golden brown, about 2 minutes per side. Repeat with any remaining oysters, adding olive oil if necessary.

Top each portion of Spicy Cabbage Salad with 5 oysters and serve immediately.

GRILLED POLENTA WITH ROASTED TOMATO SAUCE AND GORGONZOLA

SERVES SIX

Team this flavorful appetizer with Roasted Red Pepper and Lentil Soup for a vegetarian feast.

■ POLENTA

2 cups/250 mL/8 fl oz Chicken or Vegetable Stock (see page 141)
1 tablespoon chopped fresh marjoram
3 cloves garlic
5 dashes hot pepper sauce
salt and freshly ground black pepper, to taste
1 cup/155 g/5 ounces finely ground polenta (cornmeal/maize)
1 teaspoon unsalted butter

■ ROASTED TOMATO SAUCE

⅓ cup/120 mL/4 fl oz olive oil
1 tablespoon chopped fresh herbs (such as basil, rosemary, and thyme)
½ teaspoon coarsely ground black pepper
1 stalk celery, chopped
1 carrot, chopped
1 small onion, chopped
5 cloves garlic
1½ pounds/750 g tomatoes, cored
¼ cup/60 g/2 fl oz balsamic vinegar
Salt and freshly ground black pepper, to taste
½ cup/60 g/2 oz Gorgonzola cheese, crumbled

Preheat the oven to 475° F/240° C/gas mark 9.

To make the polenta, in a medium saucepan over high temperature, heat just to a boil the stock, marjoram, garlic, hot pepper sauce, salt, and pepper. Whisk in the polenta slowly so that no lumps form. Continue whisking until thick, about 5 minutes.

Grease a baking sheet with the butter. Spoon the polenta mixture onto the sheet and level it with a spatula. Set aside in the refrigerator for 1 hour.

To make the sauce, place the ½ cup/120 mL/4 fl oz olive oil, chosen herbs, pepper, celery, carrot, onion, and garlic in a roasting pan. Place the cored tomatoes on top of the vegetables and roast until the tops of the tomatoes are brown, about 45 minutes. In a food processor, puree the mixture until smooth. Add the vinegar and blend. Season with salt and pepper and set aside. (I prefer to serve the Roasted Tomato Sauce at room temperature. If you'd rather have it warm, place it in a saucepan at this point and bring it just to a simmer over low heat.)

Turn the cooled polenta out on a board and cut it into 6 triangles. Oil and heat a grill (barbecue), and cook the polenta until golden, about 2 minutes per side. (Or do this under the broiler/grill.) Place the Grilled Polenta on 6 plates and pour on the Roasted Tomato Sauce. Top with the crumbled Gorgonzola and serve immediately.

SAUTÉED PRAWNS WITH SWEET PEPPERS

SERVES FOUR

All the sweet bell peppers and crisp vegetables are so colorful in this dish. As always, go right ahead and spice things up with more chile oil, if you'd like.

    16 prawns (about 1 pound/500 g)
    2 teaspoons vegetable oil
    1 small red (Spanish) onion, julienned
    ¼ pound/120 g snow peas (mange tout)
    1 red bell pepper (capsicum), julienned
    1 yellow bell pepper (capsicum), julienned
    2 cloves garlic, chopped
    1 teaspoon chopped fresh ginger
    juice of 1 lime
    ½ teaspoon ground cumin
    5 dashes chile oil
    salt and freshly ground black pepper, to taste

Peel and devein the prawns and set aside.

In a very large sauté pan over high temperature, heat the vegetable oil until smoking hot. Add the prawns and cook until they just turn pink, 2 or 3 minutes. Add the onion, snow peas, red and yellow peppers, and garlic and sauté for 1 or 2 minutes more, until the vegetables are crisp-tender. Add the ginger, lime juice, cumin, and chile oil and toss together well. Season with salt and pepper.

Arrange the vegetables attractively on individual salad plates with a prawn placed at each point of the compass.

Serve the Sautéed Prawns with Sweet Peppers immediately.

SOUPS

- Leek Soup with Apples and Blue Cheese *23*
- Roasted Garlic and Tomato Soup *24*
- Roasted Red Pepper and Lentil Soup *25*
- Sweet Pea Soup *26*
- Asian Vegetable Soup *27*
- Curry Winter Squash Soup *28*
- Tomato Mussel Soup *29*
- Gazpacho with Chipotle Peppers *30*
- Black Bean Soup *31*
- Scallop Soup *32*

LEEK SOUP WITH
APPLES AND BLUE CHEESE
SERVES SIX

This creamy soup has a sort of nutty flavor from the sherry and a tangy bite from the apples and cheese. I often enjoy it as an entree with a green salad with Simple Vinaigrette and some Honey Wheat Bread.

    4 leeks
    2 tablespoons/30 g/1 ounce unsalted butter
    2 cloves garlic, chopped
    2 shallots, chopped
    1 medium onion, diced
    3 tart apples (such as Granny Smith), peeled and sliced
    1 cup/250 mL/8 fl oz dry sherry
    1 cup/250 mL/8 fl oz apple cider
    4 large baking potatoes, peeled and diced
    4 cups/1 L/32 fl oz Chicken or Vegetable Stock (see page 141)
    1 cup/250 mL/8 fl oz heavy (double) cream
    4 ounces/120 g blue cheese, plus 2 tablespoons for garnish
    salt and freshly ground black pepper, to taste
    slices of red apple, for garnish

Discard the green portion of the leeks. Trim and rinse the whites thoroughly, then chop.

In a large stockpot over high heat, melt the butter until it starts to bubble. Add the leeks, garlic, shallots, onion, apples, sherry, and cider and cover. Over high heat, sweat the mixture until the onions are soft and half the liquid has evaporated, about 5 minutes. Add the potatoes and stock and simmer over medium heat until the potatoes are tender, about 25 to 30 minutes. Puree the soup in a blender or in batches in a food processor.

Return the soup to the pot, add the cream, and stir. Over medium heat, bring the soup just to a boil. Add the cheese and mix thoroughly. Season to taste with salt and pepper.

Serve the Leek Soup hot in a tureen, garnished with slices of red apple and crumbled blue cheese, or in individual bowls.

ROASTED GARLIC AND TOMATO SOUP
SERVES FOUR

This is a robust, full-bodied soup that can stand on its own as a meal. It's also good as a prelude to Roast Pork with Sautéed Greens.

> 2 to 3 pounds/1 to 1.5 kg medium tomatoes
> 8 cloves garlic
> 3 shallots
> 2 sprigs rosemary, or ¼ teaspoon dried
> 1 tablespoon chopped fresh thyme, or 1 tablespoon dried
> ½ cup/120 mL/4 fl oz olive oil
> 4 cups/1 L/32 fl oz Chicken Stock (see page 141)
> ¼ cup/60 mL/2 fl oz balsamic vinegar
> 2 teaspoons chopped fresh basil, or 1 teaspoon dried
> ½ teaspoon freshly ground black pepper
> salt, to taste
> goat cheese or Parmesan cheese, for garnish

Preheat the oven to 400° F/200° C/gas mark 6.

Place the tomatoes, garlic, shallots, rosemary, and thyme in a baking dish 9 x 11 inch/ 23 x 28 cm. Cover with the olive oil. Bake until the tomatoes begin to brown, 15 to 20 minutes. Using a slotted spoon, transfer this mixture to a heavy stockpot and add one half of the liquid from the baking dish. Discard or freeze the remainder. Add the Chicken Stock and simmer over medium heat until the tomatoes and the liquid are reduced by one third, about 15 minutes.

Add the balsamic vinegar, basil, black pepper, and salt and simmer for 5 to 10 minutes. Puree in a blender or in batches in a food processor.

Strain the soup through a sieve into a tureen. Serve hot, topped with goat cheese or freshly grated Parmesan.

opposite: Chilled Shrimp with Smoked Onion Aïoli, page 3, and Tomato Bruschetta, page 7

ROASTED RED PEPPER AND LENTIL SOUP

SERVES SIX

This soup is *so* great. Make a double recipe and freeze half. That way, you'll have another wonderful meal at a moment's notice!

    1 tablespoon olive oil
    1 large onion, diced
    3 shallots, diced
    4 cloves garlic, chopped
    1 carrot, roughly chopped
    2 stalks celery, roughly chopped
    2 cups/500 g/16 ounces lentils
    8 cups/2 L/64 fl oz Chicken Stock (see page 141)
    1 ham hock (optional)
    2 red bell peppers (capsicums), roasted (see page 144) and pureed
    1 jalapeño pepper, roasted (see page 144) and pureed
    pinch curry powder
    1 teaspoon ground cumin
    1 tablespoon cayenne or chile sauce
    salt and freshly ground black pepper, to taste

In a large stockpot over high temperature, heat the olive oil until very hot. Add the onion, shallots, and garlic and sauté until they begin to give off their aroma, 2 or 3 minutes. Add the carrots, celery, and lentils and mix to coat the lentils with olive oil. Add the stock and optional ham hock and simmer until the lentils are tender, about 20 minutes.

Add the pureed red and jalapeño peppers to the soup. Add the curry, cumin, and cayenne sauce. Season with salt and pepper. If you have added the ham hock, remove it and discard; or pull the meat from the bone, chop, and add it to the soup. Bring the soup just to a boil and serve immediately.

opposite: Curry Winter Squash Soup, page 28, and Toasted Bread with Wilted Greens and Yellow Pepper Vinaigrette, page 51

SWEET PEA SOUP

SERVES SIX

It may take a while to shell the peas for this soup, but it's well worth the effort. Frozen peas will work, but they just don't have the same delicate flavor that makes this rich, creamy soup such a winner.

1 tablespoon/15 g/½ ounce unsalted butter
1 medium onion, diced
3 cloves garlic, chopped
3 shallots, chopped
1 pound/500 g fresh green peas, shelled
2 potatoes, peeled and diced
4 cups/1 L/32 fl oz Chicken Stock (see page 141)
1 cup/250 mL/8 fl oz heavy (double) cream
2 teaspoons chopped fresh tarragon, or 1 teaspoon dried
juice of 1 lemon
salt and freshly ground black pepper, to taste
Crème Fraîche (see page 143), for garnish

In a large, heavy saucepan over high heat, melt the butter. Add the onion, garlic, and shallots and sauté until they begin to give off their aroma, 2 or 3 minutes. Add the peas, diced potatoes, and stock and simmer over medium heat until the potatoes are tender, about 10 minutes.

Puree the mixture in a blender or in batches in a food processor. Pour it back into the saucepan, add the cream, and heat just to a boil. Add the tarragon and lemon juice and season with salt and pepper.

Serve immediately, topped with a little Crème Fraîche.

Asian Vegetable Soup

SERVES SIX

This easy soup is very low in fat. I like it with some of John's Sesame Noodles for an Asian-style supper. It also makes a meal in itself if you add some grilled or poached prawns to the broth and spoon it over steamed rice or couscous.

2 teaspoons peanut or vegetable oil
1 red (Spanish) onion, julienned
1 carrot, julienned
¼ pound/120 g/4 ounces snow peas (mange tout), halved on the diagonal
1 red bell pepper (capsicum), julienned
¼ pound/120 g/4 ounces bean sprouts
½ Napa (Chinese) cabbage, julienned
2 teaspoons chopped fresh ginger
3 cloves garlic, chopped
4 cups/1 L/32 fl oz Chicken Stock (see page 141)
2 teaspoons sesame oil
1 teaspoon fish sauce
1 teaspoon cayenne pepper
¼ teaspoon ground cumin
2 or 3 dashes soy sauce
freshly ground black pepper, to taste
5 green (spring) onions, chopped, for garnish

In a large saucepan or wok over high temperature, heat the oil until very hot. Add the onion and carrot and sauté until the onion is tender, 2 or 3 minutes. Add the snow peas, red pepper, bean sprouts, and cabbage and sauté for 2 more minutes. Add the ginger and garlic and toss with the vegetables.

Add the stock, sesame oil, and fish sauce and bring to a boil. Add the cayenne and cumin and season with soy sauce and black pepper. Serve immediately, garnished with green onions.

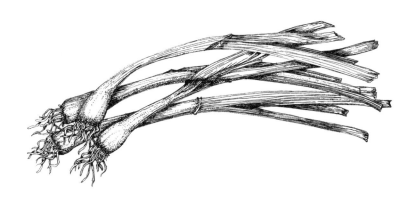

CURRY WINTER SQUASH SOUP
SERVES SIX

Winter squash makes a warming soup for the holidays, and the curry gives an especially nice dimension here. If you come home with a squash that's difficult to peel, cut it in half and remove the seeds and strings. Roast it, cut side down, for about an hour in an oven preheated to 350° F/180° C/gas mark 4. Then scoop out the flesh and add it to the soup just before you put in the coconut milk.

1 tablespoon olive oil
1 onion, diced
2 shallots, chopped
3 cloves garlic, chopped
1 tablespoon chopped fresh ginger
1 cup/250 mL/8 fl oz mirin wine or sweet cooking wine
4 pounds/2 kg winter squash, peeled and diced
3 cups/750 mL/24 fl oz Chicken Stock (see page 141)
1½ cups/375 mL/12 fl oz coconut milk
1 tablespoon curry powder
½ teaspoon chile powder
Salt and freshly ground black pepper, to taste
2 tablespoons roasted squash seeds, for garnish
2 tablespoons Crème Fraîche (see page 143), for garnish

In a large saucepan over high temperature, heat the olive oil until very hot. Add the onion, shallots, garlic, and ginger and sauté until they begin to give off their aroma, 2 or 3 minutes. Add the mirin and cook until half the liquid has evaporated, about 3 or 4 minutes. Add the diced squash and stock. Reduce the heat and simmer until the squash is tender, about 15 minutes. Add the coconut milk and continue simmering for 5 more minutes.

While the soup is simmering, place the curry powder in a small sauté pan over high heat. Dry-sauté the curry until you can smell its aroma, 1 or 2 minutes. Add it to the soup when it has finished simmering.

Puree the soup in a blender or in batches in a food processor. Add the chile powder and season to taste with salt and pepper. Serve immediately garnished with squash seeds and crème fraîche.

TOMATO MUSSEL SOUP

SERVES SIX

Basil's such a great herb for this soup, but rosemary and oregano are also good, so by all means use them if you prefer. Some chunks of potato transform an already hearty soup into a robust stew.

    3 pounds/1.5 kg mussels
    1 tablespoon olive oil
    1 medium onion, diced
    3 shallots, chopped
    4 cloves garlic, chopped
    ½ cup/120 mL/4 fl oz red wine
    5 pounds/2.5 kg tomatoes, seeded and diced
    1 tablespoon chopped fresh basil, or ½ tablespoon dried
    ½ cup/90 g/3 ounces grated Parmesan cheese
    salt and freshly ground black pepper, to taste

Debeard and scrub the mussels and set aside.

In a large saucepan over high temperature, heat the oil until very hot. Add the onion, shallots, and garlic and sauté until they begin to give off their aroma, 2 or 3 minutes. Add the mussels and red wine and cover. Steam the mussels until they open, discarding any that have not opened after 10 minutes. Remove the mussels from the pan using a slotted spoon and set them aside.

Add the diced tomatoes to the onion mixture in the saucepan. Simmer until the tomatoes start to sweeten, about 20 minutes.

Meanwhile, when the mussels are cool enough to handle, remove them from their shells. Discard the shells and set the mussels and any liquor aside.

When the tomato mixture has finished simmering, puree it in a blender or in batches in a food processor and return it to the saucepan. Add the basil, cheese, and mussels. Season with salt and pepper and bring just to a boil. Serve immediately.

GAZPACHO WITH CHIPOTLE PEPPERS

SERVES SIX

The most refreshing soup for a hot summer's day, gazpacho is a classic. The twist here is the chipotle pepper (a dried, smoked jalapeño), which gives this spicy bowlful its unusual accent.

4 large tomatoes
1 large (1 medium English) cucumber, coarsely chopped
1 red (Spanish) onion, coarsely chopped
1 red bell pepper (capsicum), seeded and coarsely chopped
3 cloves garlic, coarsely chopped
2 chipotle peppers, coarsely chopped
1 cup/250 mL/8 fl oz tomato juice
1 egg yolk
¼ cup/60 mL/2 fl oz red wine vinegar
¾ cup/175 mL/6 fl oz olive oil
pinch ground cumin
salt and freshly ground black pepper, to taste

In a food processor, chop the tomatoes, cucumber, onion, red pepper, garlic, and chipotle peppers, adding tomato juice gradually to help the process. When the mixture is a rough puree, place it in a large nonreactive bowl and set aside.

Place the egg yolk and vinegar in a small bowl and slowly whisk in the olive oil until thoroughly blended. Add the cumin. Whisk the egg mixture into the pureed vegetables and season to taste with salt and pepper. Refrigerate for several hours to allow the flavors to meld.

Serve chilled.

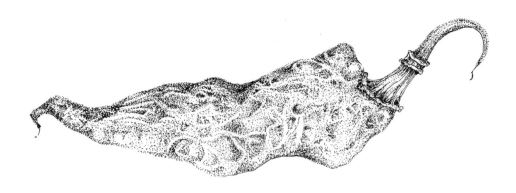

BLACK BEAN SOUP

SERVES SIX

For me, this soup is always a meal in itself. Add some crusty bread or great tortilla chips and Mocha Pots de Crème and I'm *very* happy. (By the way, if you can't find the smoked Cajun andouille sausage, substitute another of your favorite smoked sausages, or omit it entirely.)

    2 tablespoons olive oil
    1 large onion, diced
    1 stalk celery, chopped
    1 carrot, chopped
    4 cloves garlic, chopped
    1 teaspoon ground cumin
    2 cups/500 g/1 pound black beans, soaked overnight
    2 tablespoons tomato paste (puree)
    1 smoked ham hock
    8 cups/2 L/64 fl oz Chicken Stock (see page 141)
    8 ounces/250 g andouille sausage (optional)
    ½ tablespoon chipotle pepper, chopped
    ¼ cup/60 mL/2 fl oz sour cream (or crème fraîche), for garnish
    5 green (spring) onions, chopped, for garnish

In a large stockpot over medium temperature, heat the olive oil until very hot. Add the onion, celery, carrot, garlic, and cumin. Cover the pot and cook the vegetables until tender, about 5 minutes.

Drain the beans and add them to the pot. Add the tomato paste and the ham hock. Pour in sufficient stock to cover the beans. Raise the heat and bring the mixture to a boil, then simmer, uncovered, until the beans are tender, about 1 hour.

Using a slotted spoon, remove the ham hock from the soup. Pull the meat from the bone and place it in a food processor. (Discard the bone.) Add 2 cups of the broth and pulse the mixture a few times to roughly chop the meat. Transfer this mixture to a clean pot. Repeat for the remaining broth.

Cut the andouille sausage, if using, in slices ½ inch/1.5 cm thick. Add it and the chipotle pepper to the broth. Return the soup to the boil.

Ladle the soup into individual bowls and garnish with a dollop of sour cream and sprinkling of green onion.

SCALLOP SOUP

SERVES FOUR

This delicate Asian-style soup makes a delicious beginning to any meal.

    5 cups/1.25 L/40 fl oz Fish Stock (see page 140)
    2 or 3 lime leaves
    1 stalk lemon grass
    1 tablespoon olive oil
    1 small daikon radish, julienned
    2 small carrots, julienned
    1 bunch green (spring) onions, sliced
    3 cloves garlic, chopped
    1 tablespoon julienned fresh ginger
    12 large scallops
    fish sauce, to taste (optional)
    cayenne or chile sauce, to taste (optional)
    8 ounces/250 g udon noodles, cooked

In a large saucepan over high heat, bring the stock, lime leaves, and lemon grass to a boil. Reduce the heat to a simmer and cook the broth for 5 to 10 minutes until the stock is infused with flavor.

Meanwhile, heat the oil in a stockpot over medium heat. Add the daikon, carrots, green onions, garlic, and ginger until tender, about 3 minutes.

Strain the stock through a sieve into the stockpot and discard the lime leaves and lemon grass. Add the scallops and simmer until the scallops are opaque and just cooked through, about 3 minutes. Season with fish and/or cayenne sauce to taste.

Place the cooked noodles in a colander and pour boiling water over them to heat them through. Divide them among four bowls. Top each portion of noodles with 3 scallops and pour over some of the broth.

Serve the Scallop Soup immediately.

SANDWICHES

- Vegetable-Stuffed Sandwich   *35*
- Eggplant Sandwich with Roasted Red Peppers and Olive Tapenade   *36*
- Open-Faced Smoked Salmon Sandwich   *37*
- Chicken Salad Sandwich   *38*
- Grilled Pork Tenderloin Sandwich with Roasted Shallot Relish   *39*

VEGETABLE-STUFFED SANDWICH

SERVES FOUR

It's important always to use good-quality bread in your sandwiches, and this one is no exception. Snug in a loaf of French bread, it travels very well, so it's good to take on picnics. Feel free to include your favorite vegetables or even a little bit of meat, if you'd like.

1 large loaf French bread
1 small red (Spanish) onion, diced
3 red bell peppers (capsicums), roasted (see page 144) and julienned
½ cup/60 g/2 ounces water-packed artichoke hearts
2 tomatoes, seeded and diced
2 cloves garlic, chopped
¾ cup/90 g/3 ounces softened cream cheese
¼ cup/30 g/1 ounce mild soft goat cheese
1 tablespoon chopped fresh basil, or ½ tablespoon dried
salt and freshly ground black pepper, to taste

Cut the loaf in half horizontally. Remove some of the bread from the middle of each half to form a hollow.

In a small bowl, mix together the onion, red peppers, artichoke hearts, and tomatoes and set aside.

In an electric mixer, blend until smooth the garlic, cream cheese, goat cheese, basil, salt, and pepper. Add the vegetable mixture and mix until just incorporated. Spoon into the hollows in the bread and sandwich the two halves of the loaf together.

Slice into 4 portions and serve at room temperature.

Eggplant Sandwich with
Roasted Red Peppers and Olive Tapenade
SERVES FOUR

This sandwich has been on the menu since we bought our restaurant in 1992. Since then whole tables at a time have ordered it and I guess that says a lot about how great this sandwich is.

■ MARINATED EGGPLANT
1 large eggplant (aubergine)
¼ cup/60 mL/2 fl oz balsamic vinegar
2 cloves garlic, chopped
½ cup/120 mL/4 fl oz plus 2 tablespoons olive oil
1 teaspoon cracked black pepper

■ TAPENADE
¾ cup/70 g/2 ounces cured black olives, pitted
2 cloves garlic, chopped
½ teaspoon capers, drained
1 anchovy fillet
½ teaspoon lemon juice
2 tablespoons olive oil

1 medium tomato, cut into 4 slices
8 slices Honey Wheat Bread (see page 145) or other whole wheat (wholemeal) bread
1 large red bell pepper (capsicum), roasted (see page 144) and quartered
4 slices mozzarella cheese

Cut the eggplant into slices ¼ inch/0.5 cm. Place in a large nonreactive bowl and set aside.

Whisk together the vinegar, garlic, ½ cup/120 mL/4 fl oz olive oil, and cracked black pepper in a small bowl. Pour this marinade over the eggplant and set aside for 30 minutes.

Meanwhile, make the tapenade. Blend the olives, garlic, capers, and anchovy in a food processor. Add the lemon juice and the 2 tablespoons olive oil and blend to a smooth paste. Set aside.

In a large sauté pan or on griddle over high temperature, heat 1 tablespoon of the remaining olive oil until very hot. Add as many slices of marinated eggplant as will fit in the pan without crowding and sauté until brown, about 3 or 4 minutes per side. Repeat with the remaining olive oil and eggplant.

Once all the eggplant is cooked, remove with a slotted spoon and set aside. Add the tomato slices to the pan and cook until tender, about 2 minutes.

Toast all the bread and spread each slice with ½ teaspoon or so of the tapenade. Top 4 of the slices of bread with the eggplant, a slice of tomato, and a piece of roasted red pepper. Add a slice of mozzarella to each and sandwich with the remaining bread, tapenade side down.

Cut the sandwiches in half and serve immediately while still warm.

OPEN-FACED SMOKED SALMON SANDWICH

SERVES SIX

This is a beautiful sandwich to look at, with the pink of the salmon, yellow tomatoes, green of the watercress, and purplish slivers of onion. It's also a pretty beautiful sandwich to taste since John smokes the best salmon in the world. If you don't smoke your own, splurge on the best you can afford—it's worth it!

> 1⅓ pounds/670 g smoked salmon
> ⅓ cup/80 mL/3 fl oz yogurt
> ¼ cup/60 mL/2 fl oz Mayonnaise (see page 143)
> 2 cloves garlic, minced
> 2 teaspoons lemon juice
> 1 teaspoon chopped fresh lemon thyme, or ½ teaspoon dried
> salt and freshly ground black pepper, to taste
> 12 slices good-quality rye bread
> 1 bunch watercress (about 3 ounces/90 g)
> 3 large yellow tomatoes, sliced
> 1 large red (Spanish) onion, sliced

Flake the salmon into a bowl and set aside.

In another bowl, mix together the yogurt and mayonnaise. Add the garlic, lemon juice, and lemon thyme and mix well. Season with salt and pepper.

Arrange 2 slices of rye bread on each of 6 plates. Distribute the watercress over all the bread. Top with the flaked salmon, then the tomato slices. Finish with a slice of onion on each sandwich. Drizzle a generous tablespoon of the yogurt sauce over all and serve straight away.

CHICKEN SALAD SANDWICH

SERVES FOUR

Here's an elegant luncheon sandwich. If you have a ripe pear, you can use it instead of the apple, if you prefer. And if you don't care for the brie, substitute Gouda.

3 chicken half breasts
salt and freshly ground black pepper, to taste
1 tart apple (such as Granny Smith), diced
1 small red (Spanish) onion, julienned
1 stalk celery, diced
4 ounces/120 g brie cheese
½ cup/120 mL/4 fl oz Mayonnaise (see page 143)
2 tablespoons Dijon mustard
2 teaspoons chopped fresh tarragon
8 slices good-quality white bread

Preheat the oven to 350° F/175° C/gas mark 4.

Season the chicken under the skin with salt and pepper. Place in an ovenproof dish and bake for 15 minutes, or until it has an internal temperature of 150° F/75° C. Set aside to cool.

Meanwhile, mix all the other ingredients, except the bread, together well in a large bowl.

When the chicken has cooled, shred it and add to the other ingredients. Toss well to blend. Distribute among 4 slices of bread. Top with the remaining 4 slices and cut each sandwich in half.

Serve each Chicken Salad Sandwich straight away accompanied by fresh fruit.

GRILLED PORK TENDERLOIN SANDWICH
WITH ROASTED SHALLOT RELISH

SERVES FOUR

The sweet tanginess of this relish isn't just from the honey, but also from caramelizing the shallots. It goes particularly well with the pork in this hearty sandwich, but it's a versatile condiment and is also good with chicken and steak.

■ ROASTED SHALLOT RELISH
2 teaspoons olive oil
12 shallots, roughly chopped
1 teaspoon (clear) honey
¼ cup/60 mL/2 fl oz rice vinegar
¼ cup/60 mL/2 fl oz Chicken Stock (see page 141)
salt and freshly ground black pepper, to taste

1 pound/500 g pork tenderloin
2 teaspoons olive oil
salt and freshly ground black pepper, to taste
4 good-quality buns (rolls)

For the Roasted Shallot Relish, heat the olive oil until very hot in a sauté pan over high temperature. Add the shallots and cook until well browned, 5 to 10 minutes. Add the honey and vinegar and cook until the mixture is syrupy, 2 or 3 minutes. Add the stock and cook until half the liquid has evaporated, 3 or 4 minutes. Set aside to cool while you prepare the coals and the pork.

Brush the pork tenderloin with the olive oil and season with salt and pepper. Grill or barbecue the pork for 3 or 4 minutes per side for medium done. Set aside for a minute or 2 before slicing.

Distribute the pork among the buns and top with a dollop of Roasted Shallot Relish. Serve immediately.

SALADS

- Simple Vinaigrette *43*
- Sundried Tomato and Horseradish Dressing *44*
- Orange Ginger Dressing *45*
- Seasonal Greens with Spicy Lime Vinaigrette *46*
- Warm Spinach Salad with Bacon Thyme Dressing *47*
- Warm Spinach Salad with Sage and Walnut Dressing *48*
- Warm Spinach Salad with Ginger and Dried Cherry Dressing *49*
- Grilled Radicchio Salad *50*
- Toasted Bread with Wilted Greens and Yellow Pepper Vinaigrette *51*
- Bean and Tomato Salad *52*
- Asian Cole Slaw *53*
- Couscous Salad with Saffron and Currants *54*
- Yellow Fin Potato Salad with Balsamic Vinaigrette *55*

SIMPLE VINAIGRETTE

MAKES ½ CUP / 120 ML / 4 FL OZ

It's easy to make your own dressing, so here are three of my favorites to dress up your favorite greens. The first is the best standby I know for a quick, tasty salad.

    2 tablespoons white wine vinegar
    2 cloves garlic, chopped
    1 shallot, chopped
    1 teaspoon Dijon mustard
    ⅓ cup/80 mL/3 fl oz olive oil
    salt and freshly ground black pepper, to taste

Place the vinegar, garlic, shallots, and mustard in a nonreactive bowl. Whisk in the olive oil slowly to blend thoroughly. Season the vinaigrette with salt and pepper to taste. Use immediately over your favorite lettuces or greens or keep for up to 2 weeks in the refrigerator.

Sundried Tomato
and Horseradish Dressing
MAKES 1¼ CUPS / 315 ML / 10 FL OZ

A creamy dressing with a hint of pepper and flecks of sundried tomato—why ever use store-bought again when you can have a jar of this ready in the refrigerator?

2 shallots, chopped
3 cloves garlic, chopped
5 sundried tomatoes, minced
1 tablespoon grated fresh horseradish, or 2 tablespoons prepared
¼ cup/60 mL/2 fl oz red wine vinegar
1 egg yolk
½ cup/120 mL/4 fl oz olive oil
⅓ cup/80 mL/3 fl oz sour cream (or crème fraîche)
salt and freshly ground black pepper, to taste

In a food processor, blend the shallots, garlic, tomatoes, horseradish, vinegar, and egg yolk. With the motor running, add the olive oil slowly to blend thoroughly. Add the sour cream and process just until mixed. Season with salt and pepper.

Serve the Sundried Tomato and Horseradish Dressing on seasonal greens with your favorite salad garnish.

This dressing will keep about 3 weeks in the refrigerator.

ORANGE GINGER DRESSING

MAKES ABOUT 1 CUP / 250 ML / 8 FL OZ

This is our house dressing at the restaurant. We use orange juice concentrate rather than fresh orange juice for a much brighter flavor.

¼ cup/60 mL/2 fl oz rice vinegar
2 cloves garlic, chopped
1 tablespoon chopped fresh ginger
2 teaspoons orange juice concentrate
¾ cup/180 mL/6 fl oz vegetable oil
1 tablespoon sesame oil
pinch hot pepper flakes
soy sauce, to taste

In a nonreactive bowl, mix together the vinegar, garlic, ginger, and orange juice. Slowly whisk in the vegetable oil until thoroughly blended. Add the sesame oil, hot pepper flakes, and soy sauce and mix well to blend.

Use immediately, tossed over your favorite salad greens, or refrigerate for up to 2 weeks.

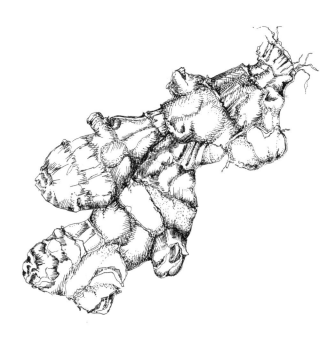

SEASONAL GREENS WITH
SPICY LIME VINAIGRETTE

SERVES SIX

Here's another great vinaigrette. Adjust the spice in this one to suit your taste.

    1 red-leaf lettuce
    1 green-leaf lettuce
    1 small radicchio
    1 small curly endive (frisée)
    1 cucumber, peeled and thinly sliced
    2 tomatoes, sliced
    6 radishes, trimmed

    ■ SPICY LIME VINAIGRETTE
    ¼ cup/60 mL/2 fl oz rice vinegar
    2 shallots, finely chopped
    2 cloves garlic, minced
    zest and juice of 1 lime
    1 teaspoon chopped fresh cilantro (coriander)
    2 teaspoons chile paste
    ¾ cup/180 mL/6 fl oz olive oil
    salt and freshly ground black pepper, to taste

Wash the leaves from the red- and green-leaf lettuces, the radicchio, and the endive and dry them thoroughly. Tear them into bite-sized pieces and toss together in a large bowl. Set aside while you prepare the Spicy Lime Vinaigrette.

Whisk together the vinegar, shallots, garlic, lime zest and juice, cilantro, and chile paste in a nonreactive bowl. Slowly whisk in the oil until it is thoroughly blended. Season to taste with salt and pepper.

Add 2 to 3 tablespoons per person of the Spicy Lime Vinaigrette to the greens and toss together well.

Arrange the dressed greens on 6 salad plates and compose the cucumber and tomato slices attractively on top. Place a radish on each salad and serve immediately.

WARM SPINACH SALAD
WITH BACON THYME DRESSING
SERVES SIX

I love warm spinach salads, so not one, but three of my favorites follow! The first is a twist on a classic with the Gouda cheese adding a whole different savor and bite.

> 2 bunches spinach (English spinach, about 1 pound/500 g)
> 6 to 8 slices pepper bacon
> 2 cloves garlic, chopped
> 1 small red (Spanish) onion, minced
> 1 tablespoon chopped fresh thyme, or ½ tablespoon dried
> 3 tablespoons balsamic vinegar
> 1 tablespoon Dijon mustard
> 3 tablespoons olive oil
> 1 teaspoon cracked black pepper
> salt, to taste
> 4 ounces/120 g Gouda cheese, cubed

Thoroughly wash, trim, and drain the spinach. Place it in a large stainless steel bowl and set aside.

In a medium sauté pan over medium heat, cook the bacon until crispy, about 15 minutes. Using a slotted spoon, remove the bacon from the pan. When cool enough to handle, crumble the bacon into small pieces and set aside.

Place the pan back on the heat and sauté the garlic and onion until they begin to give off their aroma, 2 or 3 minutes. Remove from the heat and add the thyme, vinegar, and mustard. Mix well. Add the olive oil, season with pepper and salt, and blend thoroughly.

Return the pan to the heat and bring the dressing just to a boil. Immediately pour it over the spinach, toss, and distribute among 6 salad plates.

Top with the crumbled bacon and Gouda and serve immediately while still warm.

Warm Spinach Salad
with Sage and Walnut Dressing
SERVES FOUR

Sage and walnuts aren't often paired with each other, but they work together beautifully.

■ SAGE AND WALNUT DRESSING
¼ cup/60 mL/2 fl oz sherry vinegar
2 cloves garlic, chopped
2 shallots, chopped
1 teaspoon chopped fresh sage, or ½ teaspoon dried
½ cup/120 mL/4 fl oz vegetable oil
¼ cup/60 mL/2 fl oz walnut oil
salt and freshly ground black pepper, to taste

2 bunches spinach (English spinach, about 1 pound/500 g), trimmed, washed, and drained
2 ounces/60 g blue cheese, crumbled
½ cup/60 g/2 ounces roughly chopped walnuts, toasted

In a medium bowl, whisk together the vinegar, garlic, shallots, and sage. Gradually whisk in the vegetable and walnut oils until thoroughly blended. Season to taste with salt and pepper. Transfer the Sage and Walnut Dressing to a sauté pan and bring to a boil over high heat.

Meanwhile, place the thoroughly washed and drained spinach in a large stainless steel bowl. Pour one third of the boiling dressing over the leaves and toss well. (Refrigerate the remaining dressing for up to a month.)

Distribute the Warm Spinach Salad among 4 salad plates and top each serving equally with blue cheese and toasted walnuts. Serve straight away.

WARM SPINACH SALAD WITH
GINGER AND DRIED CHERRY DRESSING
SERVES FOUR

The dried cherries in this dressing add such a rich flavor to the salad, and the ginger just a dash of welcome spice.

■ GINGER AND DRIED CHERRY DRESSING
¼ cup/50 g/1½ ounces dried cherries
2 shallots, chopped
1 tablespoon chopped fresh ginger
1 clove garlic, chopped
½ cup/120 mL/4 fl oz dry red wine
½ cup/120 mL/4 fl oz balsamic vinegar
¾ cup/180 mL/6 fl oz olive oil
½ teaspoon coarsely ground black pepper

2 bunches spinach (English spinach, about 1 pound/500 g), trimmed
1 tablespoon olive oil
1 red bell pepper (capsicum), roasted (see page 144) and sliced
¼ cup/30 g/1 ounce shiitake mushrooms, sliced
2 ounces/60 g soft, mild goat cheese, crumbled
½ small red (Spanish) onion, thinly sliced

In a saucepan over high heat, cook the cherries, shallots, ginger, garlic, wine, and vinegar until one third of the liquid remains, 3 or 4 minutes. Transfer the mixture to a food processor. With the motor running, slowly add the olive oil until thoroughly blended. Add the pepper and set the dressing aside.

Thoroughly wash and drain the spinach. Set it aside in a stainless steel bowl.

In a medium sauté pan over high temperature, heat the olive oil until very hot. Add the red pepper and mushrooms and sauté until the mushrooms are tender, about 4 minutes. Add the dressing and bring just to a boil.

Pour the dressing over the spinach and toss well. Divide among 4 salad plates and top with the goat cheese and slices of red onion. Serve immediately.

GRILLED RADICCHIO SALAD

SERVES FOUR

The pretty purplish pink radicchio, a popular salad "green" in Italy, sometimes tastes a bit too bitter, I think. Marinating then grilling makes it much milder and the perfect start to an Italian meal.

2 medium radicchio
3 cloves garlic, chopped
½ cup/120 mL/4 fl oz balsamic vinegar
½ cup/120 mL/4 fl oz olive oil
2 teaspoons cracked black pepper

Keeping the root end intact, cut the radicchio into quarters. In a large nonreactive bowl, whisk together the garlic, vinegar, olive oil, and pepper until thoroughly blended. Add the radicchio to this dressing and toss together well. Set aside for 15 to 20 minutes to allow the flavors to meld.

Meanwhile, prepare the grill (barbecue).

Using a pair of tongs, lift the radicchio from the dressing and grill for about 3 minutes on each side. During this time, it will become marked by the grill.

Roughly chop the radicchio and return to the bowl. Toss with the remaining dressing and serve immediately while still warm.

Toasted Bread with Wilted Greens and Yellow Pepper Vinaigrette

SERVES FOUR

This is both a great salad and a wonderful appetizer. Try different greens or combinations of greens to change the nature of this dish depending on your mood.

■ YELLOW PEPPER VINAIGRETTE
2 yellow bell peppers (capsicums), roasted (see page 144) and chopped
2 cloves garlic, chopped
½ medium onion, diced
½ teaspoon freshly ground black pepper
½ teaspoon dry mustard
¼ cup/60 mL/2 fl oz rice vinegar
½ cup/120 mL/4 fl oz olive oil
5 Kalamata olives, pitted and chopped
1 anchovy fillet, minced

4 large slices bread, thick, crusted, peasant-style
3 teaspoons olive oil
2 bunches arugula (rocket) or watercress (about 5 ounces/155 g)
salt and freshly ground black pepper, to taste

To make the Yellow Pepper Vinaigrette, whisk together the yellow peppers, garlic, onion, black pepper, mustard, and vinegar in a nonreactive bowl. Slowly whisk in the ½ cup/ 120 mL/4 fl oz olive oil until it is thoroughly blended. Add the olives and anchovy and stir. Set aside.

Brush the slices of bread with 2 teaspoons of the olive oil and toast until golden brown. Place on individual salad plates.

In a sauté pan over high temperature, heat the remaining olive oil until very hot. Add the arugula or watercress and sauté for between 30 seconds and 1 minute, or just until the greens wilt.

Distribute the sautéed greens among the 4 slices of toasted bread. Drizzle the vinaigrette over all and serve immediately.

BEAN AND TOMATO SALAD

SERVES FOUR

John and I take this salad on our summer picnics. You can use whatever fresh beans are in season in your area, although I like to use at least two different types for texture and flavor.

½ pound/250 g romano (Italian green) beans, trimmed
½ pound/250 g green (French) beans, preferably Blue Lake, trimmed
2 cups/500 g/16 ounces yellow cherry tomatoes, halved (1 pint)
½ cup/120 mL/4 fl oz plus 2 teaspoons olive oil
1 medium red (Spanish) onion, thinly sliced
4 cloves garlic
2 jalapeño peppers, seeded and diced
2 shallots, chopped
juice of 1 orange
juice of 1 lime
½ teaspoon ground cumin
½ teaspoon ground coriander

In a stockpot over high heat, bring 8 cups/2 L/64 fl oz of water to a boil. Add the beans and cook for 2 or 3 minutes. Drain them and plunge into a bowl of ice water to cool.

Drain the beans and transfer them to a large bowl. Add the halved tomatoes.

In a large sauté pan over medium temperature, heat the 2 teaspoons olive oil until very hot. Add the onion, garlic, jalapeño peppers, and shallots and sauté just until tender. Add this mixture to the cooled beans. Add the orange juice, lime juice, remaining olive oil, cumin, and coriander. Toss together well and refrigerate for 1 hour before serving.

ASIAN COLE SLAW
SERVES FOUR

Make this great crunchy slaw at least one hour before serving to allow the spicy orange taste time to develop.

1 small red cabbage, thinly sliced
1 small daikon radish, julienned
2 cloves garlic, chopped
1 tablespoon chopped fresh ginger
2 teaspoons orange juice concentrate
¼ cup/60 mL/2 fl oz rice vinegar
½ cup/120 mL/4 fl oz vegetable oil
1 tablespoon sesame oil
¼ teaspoon hot pepper flakes
salt and freshly ground black pepper, to taste

In a medium nonreactive bowl, toss together the cabbage and daikon radish and set aside.

To make the dressing, place the garlic, ginger, orange juice concentrate, and vinegar in another bowl. Slowly whisk in the vegetable and sesame oils until they are thoroughly blended. Add the hot pepper flakes and salt and pepper to taste. Mix well.

Add the dressing to the cabbage and toss together well. Set aside for at least 1 hour to allow the flavors to meld. Serve cold or at room temperature.

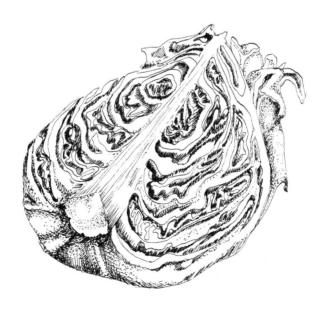

Couscous Salad
with Saffron and Currants

SERVES SIX

Couscous is a tiny pasta that has long been popular in North Africa and is *so* quick and easy to make. You can add ingredients to this list or omit items if you don't care for them, this is such an adaptable salad or side dish.

3 cups/750 mL/24 fl oz Chicken or Vegetable Stock (see page 141)
pinch saffron
salt and freshly ground black pepper, to taste
1½ cups/330 g/10 ounces couscous
1 medium red (Spanish) onion, julienned
2 cloves garlic, chopped
1 large tomato, seeded and diced
1 teaspoon chopped fresh ginger
⅓ cup/60 g/2 ounces currants
1 tablespoon chopped fresh cilantro (coriander)
juice of 2 limes
⅔ cup/155 mL/5 fl oz olive oil
salt and freshly ground black pepper, to taste

In a medium saucepan over high heat, bring the stock and saffron to a boil and season with salt and pepper. Place the couscous in a large nonreactive bowl and pour the boiling stock over it. Cover and set aside for 10 minutes, or until all the liquid has been absorbed. Fluff the couscous up with a fork and set it aside.

In a medium bowl, mix together well the onion, garlic, tomato, ginger, currants, cilantro, and lime juice. Slowly whisk in the olive oil and season with salt and pepper. Pour the mixture over the couscous and mix well.

Serve the Couscous Salad at room temperature.

Yellow Fin Potato Salad
with Balsamic Vinaigrette

SERVES FOUR

Yellow Fin potatoes are well worth the search: they're small, buttery, and finger-shaped and have much more flavor than more familiar varieties. Serving the salad warm keeps that flavor intact.

■ BALSAMIC VINAIGRETTE
¼ cup/60 mL/2 fl oz balsamic vinegar
2 shallots, chopped
2 cloves garlic, chopped
½ cup/120 mL/4 fl oz olive oil
1 teaspoon cracked black pepper
salt, to taste

2 pounds/1 kg Yellow Fin (small, creamy) potatoes
2 tablespoons olive oil
1 head garlic, roasted (see page 144)
1 red bell pepper (capsicum), roasted (see page 144) and julienned

Preheat the oven to 350° F/180° C/gas mark 4.

For the Balsamic Vinaigrette, mix together the vinegar, shallots, and garlic in a nonreactive bowl. Whisk in the ½ cup/120 mL/4 fl oz olive oil and season with cracked black pepper and salt. Set aside.

Scrub the potatoes and quarter them. In a heavy-duty sauté pan over high temperature, heat the 2 tablespoons olive oil until smoking hot. Add the potatoes and brown well. Place them in an oiled baking dish and roast until fork-tender, about 30 minutes.

Squeeze the pulp from the roasted garlic into a medium serving bowl. Add the potatoes, red pepper, and the Balsamic Vinaigrette. Toss to blend.

Serve the Yellow Fin Potato Salad warm.

ENTREES

- Steamed Salmon with Vegetable Ragoût *59*
- Poached Scallops with Riesling and Pears *60*
- Baked Halibut with Papaya Salsa *61*
- Grilled Salmon with Citrus Marinade *62*
- Seared Tuna with Eggplant Relish *63*
- Curried Glazed Prawns *64*
- Salmon with Ginger and Basil Butter Sauce *65*
- Northwest Crab Cakes with Roasted Red Pepper Aïoli *66*
- Mussel Stew with Roasted Tomatoes and Fennel *67*
- Poached Halibut in Saffron Broth *68*
- Pan-Fried Fish with Crispy Nut Crust *69*
- Sautéed Shrimp Salad *70*
- Grilled Chicken with Sweet Pepper and Olive Puree *71*
- Sautéed Chicken Breast with Apple Curry Sauce *72*
- Roasted Game Hens with Sweet Corn Salsa *73*
- Turkey Breast with Walnut and Dried Cranberry Stuffing *74*
- Chicken Breasts Stuffed with Apples and Gouda Cheese *75*
- Roast Duckling with Shiitake Fried Rice *76*
- Beef Stew with Polenta *77*
- Ossobuco with Dried Cranberries *78*
- Cured Flank Steak with Green Peppercorn Aïoli *79*
- Beef Tenderloin with Three-Peppercorn Hollandaise *80*
- Sautéed Beef Tenderloin with Arugula Pesto *81*
- Flank Steak with Asian Barbecue Sauce *82*
- N.Y. Salad with Parmesan Croutons and Black Pepper Dressing *83*
- Lamb Shanks with Wild Mushroom Sauce *84*
- Lamb Stew with Garlic Mashed Potatoes *85*
- Lamb Burgers *86*
- Roasted Leg of Lamb with Hazelnut and Gorgonzola Cream Sauce *87*
- Roast Pork with Apple Brandy Stuffing *88*
- Pork Chops with Rosemary and Dried Cherry Stuffing *89*
- Pork Tenderloin with Spicy Plum Puree *90*
- Roast Pork with Sautéed Greens and Shallot Dressing *91*
- Penne with Garlic Cream *92*
- Baked Ziti with Three Cheeses *93*
- Fettucine with Wild Mushrooms *94*
- Spicy Vegetable Stir-Fry *95*
- Pesto Pizza *96*

STEAMED SALMON WITH VEGETABLE RAGOÛT
SERVES FOUR

This dish was inspired by a visit I made to Soviet Georgia in 1988, where they serve a stew similar to the Vegetable Ragoût. Oh, the aromas this will send wafting through your house! It's also low in fat, but it sure doesn't taste like it.

■ VEGETABLE RAGOÛT
1 tablespoon olive oil
2 cloves garlic, chopped
1 red (Spanish) onion, diced
1 eggplant (aubergine), diced
⅓ pound/175 g mushrooms, sliced
1 yellow squash (or courgette), diced
1 zucchini (courgette), diced
1 red bell pepper (capsicum), diced
2 tomatoes, diced
1 tablespoon chopped fresh basil, or ½ tablespoon dried
1 teaspoon ground cumin
1½ teaspoons ground cinnamon
salt and freshly ground black pepper, to taste

2 cups/500 mL/16 fl oz water
2 cloves garlic, crushed
any leftover herb stems
1 lemon, halved
4 salmon fillets (about 6 ounces/185 g each)
salt and freshly ground black pepper, to taste
fresh basil leaves, for garnish

For the ragoût, heat the olive oil in a large sauté pan over high temperature until very hot. Add the chopped garlic and onion and cook until they begin to give off their aroma, 2 or 3 minutes. Add the eggplant and cook until golden brown, about 2 minutes. Add the mushrooms, yellow squash and zucchini, and red pepper and cook for 3 or 4 minutes, or until the vegetables are tender. Add the tomatoes, basil, cumin, and cinnamon and sauté the mixture for 2 to 3 more minutes. Season with salt and pepper and set aside, keeping the ragoût warm.

Place the water, crushed garlic, herb stems, and lemon halves in a medium saucepan. Place a bamboo steamer on top of the saucepan and heat the water just to a boil. Reduce the heat to medium. Season the salmon fillets with salt and pepper and place them in the steamer. Cover and cook until done—8 to 10 minutes for fillets 1 inch/2.5 cm thick.

Place the Steamed Salmon on a bed of the Vegetable Ragoût, garnished with fresh basil. Serve hot.

Northwest Crab Cakes
with Roasted Red Pepper Aïoli
SERVES FOUR

Well, I have to admit this is my husband John's recipe. But I can't dispute he makes great crab cakes—and neither do our customers. And if you try these, with their luscious red-pepper mayonnaise on the side, I have a feeling you'll agree.

■ ROASTED RED PEPPER AÏOLI
juice of 1 lemon
1 tablespoon Dijon mustard
¼ cup/60 mL/2 fl oz white wine vinegar
2 anchovy fillets
2 cloves garlic
3 egg yolks
1½ cups/375 mL/12 fl oz olive oil
1 red bell pepper (capsicum), roasted (see page 144)

■ CRAB CAKES
1 pound/500 g fresh crab meat
¼ cup/60 mL/2 fl oz Mayonnaise (see page 143)
½ onion, diced
2 cloves garlic, chopped
½ red bell pepper (capsicum), diced
1 tablespoon chopped fresh parsley, or ½ tablespoon dried
½ tablespoon Dijon mustard
5 dashes Worcestershire sauce
3 dashes hot pepper sauce
3 tablespoons bread crumbs
½ cup/75 g/2 ounces finely ground cornmeal
½ cup/75 g/2 ounces all-purpose (plain) flour
1 tablespoon olive oil

To make the aïoli, place the lemon juice, mustard, vinegar, anchovies, garlic, and egg yolks in a food processor. Turn the machine on and slowly add the olive oil until thoroughly blended. Add the roasted red pepper and process until smooth. Set aside.

To make the crab cakes, pick over the crab for shell and cartilage.

In a large bowl, mix together the mayonnaise, onion, garlic, diced red pepper, parsley, mustard, and Worcestershire and hot pepper sauces. Add the bread crumbs and crab meat and mix thoroughly. Form into 8 cakes.

Combine the cornmeal and flour on a plate and dredge each cake in the mixture.

In a large sauté pan over high temperature, heat the 1 tablespoon olive oil until very hot. Brown the cakes well on both sides, 2 or 3 minutes per side.

Serve the Northwest Crab Cakes hot with a dollop of Roasted Red Pepper Aïoli on the side.

MUSSEL STEW WITH
ROASTED TOMATOES AND FENNEL

SERVES SIX

Only the freshest mussels will do for this stew. Roasting the tomatoes intensifies their flavor and helps bring to this dish the deep, complex aromas and tastes we love at the restaurant. Almost any dessert in this book would do it (and your reputation!) justice.

> 10 pounds/5 kg mussels
> 8 large tomatoes, cored
> 6 cloves garlic
> ½ cup/120 mL/4 fl oz olive oil
> 2 teaspoons/10 g/⅓ ounce unsalted butter
> 1 small onion, diced
> 1 medium fennel (anise) bulb, julienned
> 1 cup/250 mL/8 fl oz red wine
> ¼ cup/60 mL/2 fl oz balsamic vinegar
> 1 teaspoon freshly ground black pepper, plus more to taste
> salt to taste

Preheat the oven to 425° F/210° C/gas mark 7.

Debeard and scrub the mussels and set aside.

Place the tomatoes and garlic in a medium baking dish. Pour over the olive oil and roast the tomatoes in the oven until their skins are blistered and brown, about 25 minutes. Remove the tomatoes and set them aside to cool.

In a very large stockpot over high temperature, heat the butter until very hot. Sauté the onion and fennel for about 2 minutes. Add the red wine and heat just to a boil. Add the mussels and cover. Steam the mussels for 7 to 10 minutes, or until they have all opened. Discard any that do not open after 10 minutes.

Coarsely chop the roasted tomatoes and garlic and add them to the mussels. Add the vinegar and teaspoon of black pepper and heat to a boil. With a slotted spoon, remove the mussels and distribute them among six bowls. Adjust the seasoning of the Roasted Tomatoes and Fennel Sauce and pour it over the mussels.

Serve the Mussel Stew straight away, accompanied by a loaf of crusty bread.

SAUTÉED CHICKEN BREAST
WITH APPLE CURRY SAUCE
SERVES FOUR

The apple in this curry sauce adds an interesting dimension that's both sweet and tart and just as delicious on fish or pork. Pair this entree with Chocolate Praline Tart?

■ APPLE CURRY SAUCE
1 teaspoon unsalted butter
2 shallots, chopped
2 cloves garlic, chopped
2 teaspoons chopped fresh ginger
1 tart apple, preferably Granny Smith, peeled and diced
½ cup/120 mL/4 fl oz dry white wine
½ cup/120 mL/4 fl oz apple cider
1 tablespoon curry powder
½ cup/120 mL/4 fl oz heavy (double) cream
salt and freshly ground black pepper, to taste

4 boneless chicken half breasts (about 5 ounces/155 g each)
salt and freshly ground black pepper, to taste
1 tablespoon olive oil
slices of red apple, for garnish
chopped green (spring) onions, for garnish

Preheat the oven to 350° F/175° C/gas mark 4.

In a large sauté pan over medium heat, melt the butter until very hot. Sauté the shallots, garlic, and ginger for about 2 minutes. Add the diced apple and toss to coat with the butter. Add the wine and cider and cook for 3 to 4 minutes, or until half the liquid has evaporated.

In a small sauté pan over high heat, dry-sauté the curry powder for 2 or 3 minutes, until it begins to give off its aroma. Add it and the cream to the apples and cook until the sauce thickens, about 5 minutes. Season to taste with salt and pepper. Set the sauce aside, keeping it warm.

Season the chicken with salt and pepper. In a large sauté pan over high temperature, heat the olive oil until smoking hot. Place the chicken breast halves skin side down in the pan and cook for 3 or 4 minutes, or until well browned. Turn the chicken over. If your sauté pan is ovenproof, place it in the oven; otherwise, transfer the chicken to a roasting pan. Bake for about 5 minutes, or until the chicken reaches an internal temperature of 155° F/80° C.

Place the chicken breasts on a serving platter and pour the Apple Curry Sauce over all. Garnish with slices of red apple and a sprinkling of chopped green onions.

opposite: Sautéed Chicken Breast with Apple Curry Sauce, this page

ROASTED GAME HENS
WITH SWEET CORN SALSA
SERVES FOUR

I really like using game hens because they cook so much more quickly than bigger chickens. Be sure to prepare the Sweet Corn Salsa at least an hour before you serve it. (You might also enjoy it with other simply prepared poultry, meat, or fish.) Mocha Pots de Crème bring your meal to a decadent conclusion.

■ SWEET CORN SALSA
1 cup/185 g/6 ounces fresh corn kernels (2 ears corn)
1 red (Spanish) onion, finely chopped
3 cloves garlic, chopped
2 red bell peppers (capsicums), roasted (see page 144) and finely chopped
juice of 1 lime
juice of 1 lemon
⅓ cup/80 mL/3 fl oz olive oil
½ teaspoon ground cumin
2 jalapeño peppers, seeded and finely chopped
1 teaspoon chopped fresh cilantro (coriander)
salt and freshly ground black pepper, to taste

4 game hens (poussins, about 1 pound/500 g each)
1 lime, halved
2 teaspoons olive oil
¼ teaspoon chile powder
¼ teaspoon ground cumin
salt and freshly ground black pepper, to taste

For the Sweet Corn Salsa, mix together well the corn kernels, onion, garlic, and red peppers in a medium nonreactive bowl. Add the lime juice, lemon juice, and olive oil and mix. Add the cumin, jalapeño peppers, cilantro, and salt and pepper to taste. Mix well and set aside for at least 1 hour to allow the flavors to blend.

Meanwhile, preheat the oven to 375° F/190° C/gas mark 5 and prepare the hens.

Place the hens in a large roasting pan and rub them all over with the cut halves of the lime. Drizzle with the olive oil. Sprinkle over the chile powder and cumin and season them to taste with salt and pepper. Roast for 20 to 25 minutes, or until the hens reach an internal temperature of 155° F/80° C. Allow the hens to rest for 2 to 3 minutes before carving.

Spoon the Sweet Corn Salsa onto a serving platter and arrange the carved game hens on top. Serve immediately.

opposite: Steamed Salmon with Vegetable Ragoût, page 59

Turkey Breast with Walnut and Dried Cranberry Stuffing

SERVES SIX

This boneless turkey breast wrapped around Walnut and Cranberry Stuffing is the ideal way to make your holiday meals a snap. What's more, it cooks in about one-third the time of a whole bird, fits in every oven, and is easy to carve. And instead of the usual pie, surprise family and friends with Pumpkin Crème Brûlée.

1 boneless turkey half breast (about 5 pounds/2.5 kg)
salt and freshly ground black pepper, to taste
½ cup/90 g/3 ounces dried cranberries
¼ cup/60 mL/2 fl oz red wine
2 tablespoons/30 g/1 ounce unsalted butter
1 medium onion, diced
3 shallots, chopped
3 cloves garlic, chopped
2 cups/120 g/4 ounces diced bread
1½ cups/375 mL/12 fl oz Chicken Stock (see page 141)
3 eggs
½ cup/60 g/2 ounces walnuts, chopped
½ teaspoon chopped fresh thyme, or ¼ teaspoon dried
¼ teaspoon chopped fresh rosemary, or ⅛ teaspoon dried
2 tablespoons olive oil

Butterfly the turkey (see page 147), and pound it slightly with a meat mallet to even the shape. Season with salt and pepper and set aside.

To make the stuffing, soak the dried cranberries in the red wine for about 30 minutes, or until the berries are soft and plump. In a large sauté pan over high temperature, heat the 2 tablespoons butter until very hot. Add the onion, shallots, and garlic and sauté until they begin to give off their aroma, 2 or 3 minutes. Add the plumped cranberries and wine and cook for 3 or 4 minutes, or until all the liquid has evaporated.

In a large bowl, toss the diced bread with the sautéed onion mixture. Add enough Chicken Stock to soften the bread. Add the eggs, walnuts, thyme, rosemary, and salt and pepper to taste and mix well. Set the stuffing aside in the refrigerator to cool completely.

Preheat the oven to 450° F/225° C/gas mark 8.

Spread the stuffing over the butterflied half breast. Roll the turkey and tie it with kitchen twine. In a large roasting pan over high heat, heat the olive oil until smoking hot. Place the turkey in the roasting pan and bake for 15 minutes, or until it is golden brown. Reduce the heat to 350° F/175° C/gas mark 4 and cook for 30 to 45 more minutes, or until the internal temperature of the turkey is 155° F/80° C.

Place on a serving platter and set aside for 2 minutes before carving into generous slices, accompanied by seasonal green vegetables.

CHICKEN BREASTS STUFFED WITH APPLES AND GOUDA CHEESE

SERVES FOUR

I love this entree. It's so easy and so different when you cut through the tender breast to the surprise stuffing of tangy cheese. Start your meal with smoky Radicchio Salad for a quick supper.

4 boneless chicken half breasts (about 5 ounces/155 g each)
3 slices bacon
3 shallots, chopped
2 cloves garlic, chopped
1 apple, diced
⅓ cup/20 g/1 ounce grated Gouda cheese
salt and freshly ground black pepper, to taste
1 tablespoon olive oil

Lay each piece of chicken flat on your work surface. Center the point of a sharp knife on the side. Make a horizontal incision 1 inch/2.5 cm long about halfway into the meat, then move the knife back and forth about 1½ inches/4 cm on either side. (The idea is to create a fan-shaped pocket, with a small opening on the side of the chicken widening out to about 3 inches/8 cm. This gives you plenty of room for stuffing, while the small opening prevents it all from falling out.) Repeat for the remaining pieces of chicken.

In a medium sauté pan over medium-high heat, cook the bacon until crispy, about 10 minutes. Remove the bacon from the pan with a slotted spoon, add the shallots and garlic, and cook until they begin to give off their aroma, 2 or 3 minutes. Add the diced apple and sauté for another minute. Set the apple mixture aside in the refrigerator to cool completely.

Preheat the oven to 350° F/175° C/gas mark 4.

Crumble the bacon and add it and the grated cheese to the cooled apple mixture. Place the stuffing in a pastry bag that has a plain tip, not a metal one. Fill the pocket of each piece of chicken with the stuffing. Season the chicken to taste with salt and pepper.

In a large sauté pan over high temperature, heat the olive oil until smoking hot. Sauté the chicken until well browned, about 2 or 3 minutes on each side. If your sauté pan is ovenproof, place it in the oven; otherwise, transfer the chicken to a baking dish. Bake for 6 to 8 minutes or until the internal temperature of the chicken reaches 155° F/80° C.

Serve the Stuffed Chicken Breast immediately accompanied by steamed broccoli or your favorite seasonal greens.

Roast Duckling with Shiitake Fried Rice

SERVES FOUR

Duck has something of a bad reputation: it's too fatty, I've heard people say, too hard to cook right. But if you follow this Asian method of steaming the bird first, then roasting it, you shouldn't have a problem. The skin will be golden brown and crispy and the meat very moist. Serve the duckling on top of the Shiitake Fried Rice for an excellent dish to celebrate family, friends, and life.

2 ducks (about 3 pounds/1.5 kg each)
salt and freshly ground black pepper, to taste
¼ cup/30 g/1 ounce black tea leaves (such as Oolong or jasmine)
3 cups/750 mL/24 fl oz water

■ SHIITAKE FRIED RICE
1 tablespoon vegetable oil
1 tablespoon chopped fresh ginger
2 cloves garlic, chopped
⅓ pound/170 g shiitake mushrooms, sliced
2 cups/400 g/12 ounces cooked long-grain rice
1 egg, beaten
1 tablespoon sesame oil
2 to 3 tablespoons soy sauce

Preheat the oven to 375° F/190° C/gas mark 5.

Sprinkle the ducks with salt and pepper. Place a rack in a large roasting pan and pour in the tea and water. Place the ducks on the rack and cook for about 20 minutes. Remove the pan from the oven. Remove the ducks and discard the liquid. Place the ducks back on the rack and roast for 45 more minutes, until the ducks are golden brown, or reach an internal temperature of 155° F/80° C.

While the ducks are cooking, prepare the rice.

In a large sauté pan over high temperature, heat the vegetable oil until very hot. Add the ginger and garlic and sauté until they begin to give off their aroma, 2 or 3 minutes. Add the mushrooms and sauté until tender, about 3 minutes. Add the cooked rice and sauté for 2 or 3 more minutes, or until the rice is hot. Add the beaten egg and cook just until the egg is set. Add the sesame oil and soy sauce and mix well. Cover and set aside.

Remove the ducklings from the oven and set aside for 2 minutes before carving.

Serve each person a drumstick and several slices of breast meat, accompanied by the Shiitake Fried Rice.

BEEF STEW WITH POLENTA

SERVES FOUR

When John and I cook together at home on a rainy Sunday (and there are a lot of them in Oregon), we often enjoy Beef Stew. It just makes you feel so warm and cosy—such a nice feeling after a hard week at the restaurant. When Mark, our lunch cook, came up with the idea of adding the polenta, our Beef Stew was turned into the best comfort food you could have.

2 pounds/1 kg beef stew meat
1 tablespoon olive oil
1 tablespoon all-purpose (plain) flour
4 cups/1 L/32 fl oz Beef or Vegetable Stock (see page 139 or page 141)
1 medium onion, diced
3 potatoes, diced
2 carrots, diced
4 cloves garlic, chopped
2 cups/500 mL/16 fl oz Vegetable or Chicken Stock (see page 141)
2 shallots, chopped
¾ cup/120 g/4 ounces finely ground polenta (cornmeal/maize)
salt and freshly ground black pepper, to taste
1 tablespoon chopped fresh thyme, or ½ tablespoon dried
1 teaspoon freshly ground black pepper
sprigs of thyme, for garnish

Trim the excess fat from the stew meat. In a large stockpot over high temperature, heat the olive oil until smoking hot. Add the beef and brown well on all sides, about 2 minutes per side. Add the flour and cook for about 2 minutes. Briskly stir in the 4 cups/1 L/32 fl oz Beef Stock thoroughly. Add the onion, potatoes, carrots, and garlic and cook over low heat for 45 minutes to 1 hour, or until the beef is tender.

About 10 minutes before the beef has finished cooking, prepare the polenta. In a heavy saucepan over high heat, bring the 2 cups/500 mL/16 fl oz Vegetable Stock and shallots to a boil. Whisk in the polenta slowly so that no lumps form. Season with salt and pepper to taste. Cook the polenta about 3 minutes, or until it becomes very thick. Stir it well to avoid scorching the bottom. Remove the pan from the heat, cover, and set aside.

When the stew has finished cooking, add the thyme, 1 teaspoon pepper, and salt to taste.

Divide the polenta among 4 bowls and ladle the stew on top. Serve immediately, garnished with sprigs of fresh thyme.

Ossobuco with Dried Cranberries

SERVES FOUR

The dried cranberries in this dish give the rich sauce a sweet, tangy accent. Braise the veal shanks slowly so they come to the table tender and juicy. Then finish this dinner off with Apple Almond Bread Pudding, one of the restaurant's famous desserts.

4 veal shanks (about 10 ounces/315 g each)
½ cup/75 g/2 ounces all-purpose (plain) flour
2 tablespoons olive oil
6 cloves garlic
2 cups/500 mL/16 fl oz Veal or Chicken Stock (see page 139 or page 141)
¾ cup/135 g/4 ounces dried cranberries
2 teaspoons chopped fresh thyme, or 1 teaspoon dried
2 teaspoons coarsely ground black pepper
salt, to taste

Preheat the oven to 350° F/175° C/gas mark 4.

Dredge the veal shanks in the flour, coating them on all sides. Shake off the excess flour. Place the olive oil in a medium roasting pan and heat it over high heat on the stove until smoking hot. Add the veal shanks and brown well on all sides, about 2 minutes per side. Add the garlic and sauté for 1 or 2 more minutes. Add the stock. Sprinkle the cranberries, thyme, and pepper over all.

Braise the veal, covered, in the oven for 1 to 1½ hours, or until tender. Salt the veal to taste.

Serve with steamed couscous or potatoes and spoon over cranberry sauce.

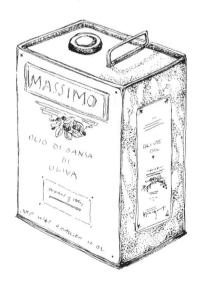

CURED FLANK STEAK
WITH GREEN PEPPERCORN AÏOLI
SERVES FOUR

M_y husband John's cure for flank steak adds such an incredible amount of flavor! Just remember flank steak should never be cooked beyond medium-rare or it will get *very* tough and all that superb savor will be wasted. Serve this with the Couscous Salad.

2 cups/375 g/12 ounces brown sugar
1 cup/120 g/4 ounces kosher salt
3 tablespoons ground mace
3 tablespoons ground allspice
3 tablespoons onion powder
3 tablespoons garlic powder
1½ tablespoons ground cloves
1 flank steak (about 2 pounds)
1 tablespoon olive oil

■ GREEN PEPPERCORN AÏOLI
1 cup/250 mL/8 fl oz plus 1 teaspoon olive oil
8 green (spring) onions
juice of 1 lemon
1 tablespoon Dijon mustard
¼ cup/60 mL/2 fl oz white wine vinegar
2 anchovy fillets
2 cloves garlic
3 egg yolks
1 tablespoon green peppercorns

Place the sugar, salt, mace, allspice, onion and garlic powders, and cloves in a food processor and blend thoroughly to make a cure for the steak. Rub the cure generously all over the steak and set aside in the refrigerator for 24 hours.

Rinse the cure off the steak and set it aside for 10 minutes to air dry.

For the aïoli, heat the 1 teaspoon olive oil until smoking hot in a medium sauté pan over high temperature. Add the green onions and sauté until charred on both sides. Set aside.

In a food processor, place the lemon juice, mustard, vinegar, anchovies, garlic, and egg yolks. Turn the machine on and slowly add the remaining olive oil until thoroughly blended. Turn the machine off and add the green onions and peppercorns. Pulse a few times to blend.

Preheat the oven to 425° F/220° C/gas mark 7.

In a large sauté pan over high temperature, heat the 1 tablespoon olive oil until smoking. Sear the steak, 2 or 3 minutes per side. If your pan is ovenproof, place it in the oven; otherwise, transfer the steak to a roasting pan. Roast for 10 to 12 minutes for medium-rare.

Set the steak aside for 2 minutes before slicing onto dinner plates and serving with a dollop of Green Peppercorn Aïoli on the side.

BEEF TENDERLOIN WITH
THREE-PEPPERCORN HOLLANDAISE
SERVES TWO

If you're going to the expense of making beef tenderloin, it'd better be for someone very special, so here's a delicious dinner just for two. The peppercorns in the hollandaise give this classic sauce a neoclassic punch. Cool your palate with a goblet of Coffee Granita.

    2 beef tenderloins (fillet steaks, about 6 ounces/185 g each)
    salt and freshly ground black pepper, to taste
    ½ teaspoon green peppercorns
    ½ teaspoon black peppercorns
    ½ teaspoon pink peppercorns
    ¼ cup/60 mL/2 fl oz white wine
    ¼ cup/60 mL/2 fl oz dry sherry
    3 tablespoons sherry vinegar
    1 shallot, chopped
    2 cloves garlic, chopped
    2 egg yolks
    ⅓ cup/90 g/3 ounces unsalted butter, melted
    1 tablespoon olive oil
    chopped flat-leaf (Italian) parsley, for garnish

Preheat the oven to 350° F/175° C/gas mark 4.

Season the tenderloins with salt and pepper and set them aside.

In a small saucepan over high heat, bring the green, black, and pink peppercorns, white wine, sherry, sherry vinegar, shallot, and garlic to a boil. Cook for about 2 minutes, or until about 2 tablespoons of liquid remain. Set aside to cool.

Place the egg yolks and the cooled wine mixture in a small stainless steel bowl. Place the bowl over a pot of simmering water and whisk for 3 to 4 minutes, or until the egg yolks thicken to the consistency of softly whipped cream. Do not scramble the eggs. Slowly whisk in the melted butter and mix thoroughly. Season to taste with salt.

Leave the bowl over the hot water and remove the pot from the heat. Cover and set aside.

In a medium sauté pan over high temperature, heat the 1 tablespoon olive oil until smoking hot. Sear the tenderloins well on both sides, about 2 minutes per side. If your sauté pan is ovenproof, place it in the oven; otherwise, transfer the beef to a roasting pan. Bake the tenderloins for about 8 minutes for medium-rare.

Place the tenderloins on individual plates and pour over the Three-Peppercorn Hollandaise. Garnish with the chopped parsley.

SAUTÉED BEEF TENDERLOIN WITH ARUGULA PESTO

SERVES FOUR

Here's another twist on a classic sauce to go with beef. Arugula is one of my favorite greens, and its nutty, slightly bitter taste works well with the nuts and garlic in pesto instead of the usual basil. It's also good on mild, firm-fleshed white fish such as sea bass.

2 bunches arugula (rocket, about 5 ounces/155 g)
3 cloves garlic
½ cup/60 g/2 ounces walnuts or pine nuts (kernels)
⅔ cup/120 g/4 ounces grated Parmesan cheese
about ⅓ cup/80 mL/3 fl oz olive oil, plus 1 tablespoon
salt and freshly ground black pepper, to taste
4 beef tenderloins (fillet steaks, about 5 ounces/155 g each)
chopped flat-leaf (Italian) parsley, for garnish

Preheat the oven to 375° F/190° C/gas mark 5.

To make the pesto, place the arugula and garlic in a food processor and pulse a few times. Add the nuts and ¼ cup/45 g/1 ounce of the Parmesan and process to chop the mixture coarsely. With the machine running, drizzle in enough of the olive oil to form a smooth paste. Season with salt and pepper and set aside.

To prepare the tenderloins, season them with salt and pepper. Heat the 1 tablespoon olive oil in a large sauté pan over high temperature and sear the beef well, 2 to 3 minutes per side. If your sauté pan is ovenproof, place it in the oven; otherwise, transfer the tenderloins to a roasting pan. Bake for 6 to 8 minutes for medium-rare.

Serve the tenderloins on dinner plates and spoon about 2 tablespoons of the Arugula Pesto onto each. Top all the portions with some of the remaining Parmesan and a scattering of flat-leaf parsley and serve immediately.

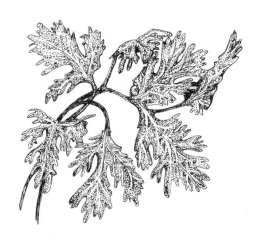

FLANK STEAK WITH ASIAN BARBECUE SAUCE

SERVES FOUR

Even though the days of inexpensive flank steak are over, it's still one of my favorite cuts of meat. Add this piquant Barbecue Sauce and a good bottle of Zinfandel and you have the makings of a sensational summer barbecue with the best of friends.

1 flank steak (about 2 pounds/1 kg)
salt and freshly ground black pepper, to taste

■ ASIAN BARBECUE SAUCE
1 tablespoon vegetable oil
2 cloves garlic, chopped
1 small onion, minced
1 tablespoon chopped fresh ginger
¼ cup/60 mL/2 fl oz mirin wine or sake
¼ cup/45 g/1 ounce brown sugar
¼ cup/60 mL/2 fl oz hoisin sauce
¼ cup/60 mL/2 fl oz rice vinegar
¼ cup/60 mL/2 fl oz tomato puree
soy sauce, to taste
½ teaspoon hot pepper flakes

Season the steak with salt and pepper and set aside.

To make the sauce, heat the vegetable oil in a medium saucepan over high temperature. Add the garlic, onion, and ginger and sauté until they begin to give off their aroma, 2 or 3 minutes. Add the mirin and brown sugar and cook for 2 to 3 minutes, or until half the liquid has evaporated. Add the hoisin, vinegar, and tomato puree. Simmer the mixture on low heat for another 5 minutes, or until it thickens and coats the back of a spoon. Season with the soy sauce and hot pepper flakes. Rub the steak with about 2 tablespoons of the barbecue sauce. Set the steak aside in the refrigerator for 30 minutes.

Place the steak on the prepared grill (barbecue) and baste with the barbecue sauce while cooking. Cook the steak about 4 minutes on each side for medium-rare; no longer, or it will get tough.

Set the steak aside for 2 minutes before slicing. Then serve on dinner plates accompanied by little dishes of the remaining barbecue sauce for dipping—and plenty of napkins!

NEW YORK SALAD WITH PARMESAN CROUTONS AND BLACK PEPPER DRESSING

SERVES SIX

This salad works equally well as a dinner or lunch entree and is an economical way of enjoying steak that's as easy on your pocketbook as it is on your palate. The best part of it, though, is the big homemade croutons!

■ STEAK SALAD
1½ pounds/750 g New York steak (sirloin)
salt and freshly ground black pepper, to taste
2 teaspoons olive oil
2 heads romaine (Cos) lettuce

■ PARMESAN CROUTONS
¼ cup/60 mL/2 fl oz olive oil
2 cups/120 g/4 ounces diced French bread
3 cloves garlic, chopped
1 teaspoon chopped fresh herbs (such as basil, rosemary, and thyme)
¼ cup/45 g/1½ ounces grated Parmesan cheese

■ BLACK PEPPER DRESSING
¼ cup/60 mL/2 fl oz balsamic vinegar
2 shallots, chopped
2 cloves garlic, chopped
½ cup/120 mL/4 fl oz olive oil
2 teaspoons cracked black pepper
⅓ cup/60 g/2 ounces grated Parmesan cheese
salt, to taste

Season the steak with salt and pepper. In a medium sauté pan over high temperature, heat the 2 teaspoons olive oil until smoking hot. Sear the steak on both sides, 3 to 4 minutes per side for medium-rare. Set aside.

To make the Parmesan Croutons, heat the ¼ cup/60 mL/2 fl oz olive oil in a large nonstick sauté pan over medium heat. Add the diced bread and toss to coat with the oil. Add the garlic and chosen herbs and sauté for 2 to 3 minutes, or until the bread starts to brown. Add the ¼ cup/45 g/1½ ounces Parmesan and sauté just until the cheese begins to melt. Set aside.

To make the Black Pepper Dressing, mix the vinegar, shallots, and garlic in a medium nonreactive bowl. Slowly whisk in the ½ cup/120 mL/4 fl oz olive oil and blend thoroughly. Add the pepper and cheese and mix well. Season with salt and set aside.

Tear the romaine leaves into a large bowl. Add about ½ cup/120 mL/4 fl oz of the Black Pepper Dressing and toss well. Divide the lettuce among six plates. Slice the steak and arrange in a fan on top of the greens. Top each serving with the Parmesan Croutons.

LAMB SHANKS WITH
WILD MUSHROOM SAUCE

SERVES FOUR

In the Pacific Northwest, we're lucky to have wild mushrooms in abundance. Their rich flavor and texture pair especially well with slowly braised lamb shanks. Make the most of the autumn harvest with Poached Pear Tart to follow. What a great meal for a chilly fall evening!

4 lamb shanks (about 1 pound/500 g each)
1 cup/155 g/5 ounces all-purpose (plain) flour, for dusting
1 tablespoon olive oil
4 cloves garlic, chopped
1 pound/500 g wild mushrooms (such as shiitake, oyster, or chanterelle)
½ cup/120 mL/4 fl oz red wine
2 cups/500 mL/16 fl oz Lamb Stock (see page 139)
1 teaspoon chopped fresh rosemary, or ½ teaspoon dried
1 teaspoon chopped fresh savory, or ½ teaspoon dried
salt and freshly ground black pepper, to taste

Preheat the oven to 350° F/175° C/gas mark 4.

Dredge the lamb shanks in the flour and set them aside.

In a roasting pan on the stove over high heat, heat the olive oil until smoking hot. Add the lamb shanks and brown them well, 4 or 5 minutes per side. Add the garlic and mushrooms and sauté until the mushrooms are tender, 3 or 4 minutes. Add the wine and cook for another 3 or 4 minutes, or until half the wine has evaporated. Add the stock and bring the mixture to a boil over high heat. Add the rosemary, savory, and salt and pepper to taste.

Cover the roasting pan with a lid or aluminum foil and place it in the oven. Bake until the lamb is tender, 1 to 1½ hours.

Serve the Lamb Shanks with the Wild Mushroom Sauce and accompanied by rice.

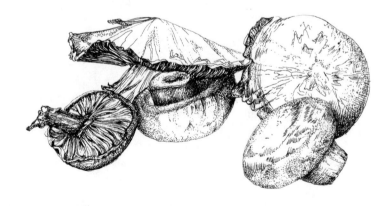

LAMB STEW WITH
GARLIC MASHED POTATOES
SERVES SIX

If I had to pick just one vegetable for the rest of my life, it would be potatoes. Add some garlic and I'm in heaven. If the Beef Stew with Polenta is a dish for the dark days of winter, this is one to celebrate the coming of spring, so leave the skin on the new potatoes. And if you can get your hands on some early berries, serve Strawberry Streusel to finish.

3 pounds/1.5 kg lamb stew meat
1 tablespoon olive oil
8 cloves garlic
1 small onion, diced
1 large turnip (swede), diced
2 carrots, diced
1 cup/250 mL/8 fl oz red wine
5 cups/2.5 L/40 fl oz Lamb or Vegetable Stock (see page 139 or page 141)
sprigs of rosemary, for garnish

■ GARLIC MASHED POTATOES
1 pound/500 g new potatoes
5 cloves garlic
⅓ cup/80 mL/2 fl oz heavy (double) cream
1 tablespoon/15 g/½ ounce unsalted butter
salt and freshly ground black pepper, to taste
1 teaspoon chopped fresh rosemary, or ½ teaspoon dried
1 teaspoon chopped fresh marjoram, or ½ teaspoon dried
salt and freshly ground black pepper, to taste

Trim the excess fat off the stew meat. In a large saucepan over high temperature, heat the olive oil until smoking hot. Add the lamb and the 8 cloves garlic and brown the lamb well, about 2 minutes per side. Add the onion, turnip, carrots, and red wine and boil for 3 to 4 minutes, or until about ½ cup/120 mL/4 fl oz of the liquid remains. Add the stock and simmer for 45 minutes to 1 hour, or until the lamb is tender.

After the lamb has been cooking for about 20 minutes, prepare the Garlic Mashed Potatoes. Place the potatoes and 5 cloves garlic in a large saucepan and cover them with water. Boil the potatoes about 30 minutes, or until tender, then drain them. Return the potatoes to the pot and mash well. Add the cream and butter and mix well. Season with salt and pepper and keep warm.

When the lamb is tender, add the rosemary, marjoram, and salt and pepper to taste.

Divide the Garlic Mashed Potatoes among 6 bowls. Ladle the Lamb Stew over the potatoes and garnish with fresh sprigs of rosemary. Serve hot.

LAMB BURGERS

SERVES FOUR

I know as a chef I'm supposed to eat exotic food, but I'll admit there's nothing better than a great hamburger—except a great lamb burger. Serve these topped with mild goat cheese and Herbed Oven-Roasted Fries on the side.

2 pounds/1 kg ground lamb
1 generous tablespoon olive oil
1 small onion, minced
3 cloves garlic, chopped
¼ cup/30 g/1 ounce bread crumbs
½ teaspoon chopped fresh rosemary, or ¼ teaspoon dried
2 tablespoons cayenne or chile sauce
salt and freshly ground black pepper, to taste

Place the ground lamb in a large bowl.

In a small sauté pan over high temperature, heat about 1 teaspoon of the olive oil until very hot. Add the onion and garlic and sauté until they begin to give off their aroma, 2 or 3 minutes. Set aside to cool.

Add the cooled onion mixture, bread crumbs, rosemary, cayenne sauce, and salt and pepper to the ground lamb and mix thoroughly. Form into 4 burgers.

In a medium sauté pan over high temperature, heat the remaining olive oil until smoking hot. After 1 minute, turn the heat to medium. Cook the burgers about 3 minutes on each side for medium, or as long as you prefer.

Top with a mild fresh goat cheese or your favorite cheese. Serve the Lamb Burgers on good-quality buns accompanied by your choice of condiments.

ROASTED LEG OF LAMB WITH
HAZELNUT AND GORGONZOLA CREAM SAUCE
SERVES SIX

This recipe takes a bit more time to prepare than others in the book, but it's worth every minute. It's so delicious. Pair it with an easy dessert such as Champagne Fruit Compote.

1 boneless leg of lamb (about 3 pounds/1.5 kg)
6 cloves garlic, roasted (see page 144)
4 shallots, roasted (see page 144)
½ tablespoon freshly ground black pepper
2 tablespoons chopped fresh herbs (such as thyme, sage, and rosemary)
2 tablespoons olive oil
2 teaspoons salt
1 tablespoon balsamic vinegar
1 onion, chopped
1 carrot, chopped
1 stalk celery, chopped

■ HAZELNUT AND GORGONZOLA SAUCE
2 shallots, chopped
½ cup/120 mL/4 fl oz white wine
2 tablespoons hazelnut liqueur
1 cup/250 mL/8 fl oz heavy (double) cream
¼ cup/30 g/1 ounce toasted hazelnuts, chopped
1 teaspoon chopped fresh rosemary
2 generous tablespoons Gorgonzola cheese
salt and freshly ground black pepper, to taste

Preheat the oven to 500° F/250° C/gas mark 9. Roll the leg of lamb so that the grain is running the length of the meat. Tie the lamb securely with kitchen twine and set aside.

Squeeze the pulp from the garlic and shallot into a food processor. Add the black pepper, chosen herbs, olive oil, salt, and vinegar and blend until smooth. Rub the mixture on the leg of lamb to coat it thickly. Set aside.

In a medium roasting pan, place the chopped onion, carrot, and celery and lay the lamb on the vegetables. Bake the lamb for 15 minutes, or until slightly browned. Turn the heat to 350° F/175 ° C/gas mark 4 and bake for 30 to 45 more minutes, or until the internal temperature of the lamb is 135° F/70° C for medium-rare.

About 10 minutes before the lamb is due to come out of the oven, prepare the sauce. In a saucepan over medium temperature, heat the shallots, wine, and liqueur for 3 to 4 minutes, or until almost all the liquid has evaporated. Add the cream and cook until it starts to thicken, about 5 minutes. Add the chopped hazelnuts and cook for 2 more minutes. Add the rosemary and Gorgonzola cheese and mix well. Season with salt and pepper.

Set the lamb aside for 2 minutes before slicing with the Cream Sauce on the side.

ROAST PORK WITH APPLE BRANDY STUFFING

SERVES SIX

Pork and apples are a classic combination, with the cider and brandy adding a new dimension. You can mix the apples with another dried fruit, if you'd prefer, or even substitute another fruit entirely: dried pears with pear juice and calvados instead of the cider and brandy, for instance. I'd like to follow this with Raspberry Port Ice Cream.

1 pork roast (about 3 pounds/1.5 kg)
2 tablespoons olive oil
1 onion, diced
2 shallots, minced
3 cloves garlic, chopped
1 apple, sliced
½ cup/90 g/3 ounces dried apples
¼ cup/60 mL/2 fl oz apple cider
¼ cup/60 mL/2 fl oz apple brandy
1 cup/60 g/2 ounces diced bread
¼ cup/60 mL/2 fl oz Chicken Stock (see page 141)
1 egg, beaten
salt and freshly ground black pepper, to taste

Trim most of the fat off the pork roast and butterfly it (see page 147). Pound the pork slightly with a meat mallet to even the shape. Set aside in the refrigerator.

In a medium sauté pan over high temperature, heat 1 tablespoon of the olive oil until very hot. Sauté the onion, shallots, and garlic until they begin to give off their aroma, 2 or 3 minutes. Add the fresh and dried apples and sauté for another minute. Add the cider and brandy and cook until half the liquid has evaporated, about 3 or 4 minutes. Transfer to a medium bowl and set aside in the refrigerator to cool.

When the mixture has cooled, add the diced bread. Add the stock and mix well to soften the bread. Add the egg, salt, and pepper, and blend thoroughly. Set aside in the refrigerator to cool completely.

Preheat the oven to 475° F/240° C/gas mark 9.

Lay the butterflied pork out on a cutting board and spread with the stuffing. Roll the pork up, tie with kitchen twine at intervals about ½ inch/1.5 cm, and season to taste.

Place the remaining olive oil in a roasting pan, and heat the pan in the oven until the oil is smoking hot. Place the roast in the pan and bake for about 5 minutes, or until well browned. Then turn the roast over and cook for another 5 minutes to brown the other side. Lower the heat to 350° F/175° C/gas mark 4 and cook for 30 to 35 more minutes, or until the roast reaches an internal temperature of 150° F/75° C. Set the roast aside for a few minutes before slicing.

Place the sliced Roast Pork on a platter, accompanied by seasonal greens.

opposite: New York Salad with Parmesan Croutons and Black Pepper Dressing, page 83

PORK CHOPS WITH ROSEMARY AND DRIED CHERRY STUFFING

SERVES FOUR

Comfort food for the nineties ... Gone are plain old overcooked pork chops! This juicy preparation followed by Cinnamon Rum Flan is one of the cosiest dinners you'll ever eat.

4 double-thick pork chops (about 10 ounces/315 g each)
2 tablespoons olive oil
½ onion, minced
2 cloves garlic, chopped
¼ cup/45 g/1 ounce dried cherries
¼ cup/60 mL/2 fl oz red wine
2 cups/120 g/4 ounces diced bread
¼ cup/60 mL/2 fl oz Chicken or Vegetable Stock (see page 141)
1 egg, beaten
1 teaspoon chopped fresh rosemary, or ½ teaspoon dried
salt and freshly ground black pepper, to taste
1 cup/155 g/5 ounces all-purpose (plain) flour, seasoned with salt and pepper to taste

Lay each pork chop flat on your work surface. Center the point of a sharp knife on the fatty side. Make a horizontal incision 1 inch/2.5 cm long through the fat and into the meat. When the knife is about halfway into the chop, move it back and forth about 1½ inches/4 cm on either side. (The idea is to create a fan-shaped pocket, with a small opening widening out to about 3 inches/8 cm. This gives you plenty of room for stuffing, while the small opening prevents it all from falling out.) Repeat for the remaining chops.

In a sauté pan over high temperature, heat 2 teaspoons of the olive oil until very hot. Add the onion and garlic and sauté until they begin to give off their aroma, about 2 minutes. Add the cherries and wine and heat just to a boil. Transfer to a large nonreactive bowl.

Add the diced bread and toss. Set aside in the refrigerator to cool completely.

Add the stock and the egg to the cooled bread mixture and mix until the bread is well moistened. Add the rosemary, salt, and pepper. Set the stuffing aside in the refrigerator.

Preheat the oven to 350° F/175° C/gas mark 4.

Place the stuffing in a piping bag that has a plain tip, not a metal one. Fill each of the pockets with the stuffing. Dredge the pork chops in the seasoned flour.

In a very large sauté pan over high temperature, heat the remaining olive oil until smoking hot. Brown the chops well on both sides, about 2 minutes per side. If your sauté pan is ovenproof, place it in the oven; otherwise, transfer the chops to a roasting pan. Bake for 20 to 25 minutes, or until the temperature of the stuffing reaches 150° F/75° C.

Serve the pork chops with roasted potatoes and vegetables.

opposite: Pesto Pizza, page 96

PORK TENDERLOIN WITH SPICY PLUM PUREE

SERVES FOUR

Serve this dish at the height of plum season—it's such an easy entree. When you pair it with John's Sesame Noodles, you've got a quick, unusual dinner to impress your guests with Asian flair.

    4 pork tenderloins (about 5 ounces/155 g each)
    ¼ teaspoon ground cumin
    pinch chile powder
    salt and freshly ground black pepper, to taste
    2 teaspoons/10 g/⅓ ounce unsalted butter
    2 shallots, chopped
    2 cloves garlic, chopped
    2 jalapeño peppers, seeded and chopped
    1 cup/250 mL/8 fl oz red wine
    2 pounds/1 kg fresh black plums, pitted and coarsely chopped
    1 tablespoon olive oil
    sprigs of cilantro (coriander), for garnish
    plum slices, for garnish

Trim the excess fat off the tenderloins. Season them with the cumin, chile powder, and salt and pepper. Set aside.

Preheat the oven to 350° F/175° C/gas mark 4.

To make the puree, in a large saucepan over medium temperature, heat the butter until very hot. Add the shallots and garlic and sauté until they begin to give off their aroma, 2 or 3 minutes. Add the jalapeños and toss to coat with the butter. Add the wine and chopped plums and cook until the plums are tender, about 5 minutes. In a food processor, puree the mixture until smooth. Return the puree to the saucepan and season with salt and pepper. Keep warm while you cook the pork.

In a large sauté pan over high temperature, heat the olive oil until smoking hot. Sear the tenderloins well, about 2 minutes per side. If your sauté pan is ovenproof, place the tenderloins in the oven; otherwise, transfer the tenderloins to a roasting pan. Bake the pork for 8 to 10 minutes, or until each tenderloin reaches an internal temperature of 150° F/75° C.

Set them aside for 2 minutes before slicing thinly on an angle.

Pour the Spicy Plum Puree on the bottom of a serving platter and arrange the pork on top, or reserve some of the puree for serving on the side. Garnish with cilantro and plum slices and serve straight away.

ROAST PORK WITH SAUTÉED GREENS AND SHALLOT DRESSING

SERVES SIX

Here's another new twist on an old favorite. This dish has so many different flavors—the greens with their peppery spice, the shallots sweet and rich—all the perfect complement to the tender pork. Orange Crème Brûlée is a memorable dessert for this entree.

1 pork roast (about 3 pounds/1.5 kg)
salt and freshly ground black pepper, to taste
1 tablespoon olive oil

■ SHALLOT DRESSING
8 shallots, roasted (see page 144) and chopped
3 tablespoons sherry vinegar
2 cloves garlic, chopped
1 tablespoon Dijon mustard
½ cup/120 mL/4 fl oz olive oil, plus 1 teaspoon for sautéing
salt and freshly ground black pepper, to taste
2 bunches mustard greens or spinach (English spinach, about 1 pound/500 g)

Preheat the oven to 425° F/210° C/gas mark 7.

Season the pork roast with salt and pepper. Place a roasting pan in the oven with 1 tablespoon olive oil until smoking hot. Add the roast and brown well, about 10 minutes. Reduce the heat to 350° F/175° C/gas mark 4 and cook for 25 more minutes, or until the roast reaches an internal temperature of 150° F/75° C.

While the roast is cooking the additional 25 minutes, mix together the shallots, sherry vinegar, garlic, and mustard in a medium nonreactive bowl. Slowly whisk in the ½ cup/ 120 mL/4 fl oz olive oil until thoroughly blended. Season with salt and pepper to taste and set aside.

Remove the roast from the oven and set aside for 2 minutes.

In a small sauté pan over high temperature, heat the 1 teaspoon olive oil until smoking hot. Add the greens and sauté for 30 seconds to a minute, or just until they begin to wilt. Place the greens on a serving platter.

Slice the Roast Pork and place on the bed of greens and drizzle over the Shallot Dressing.

PENNE WITH GARLIC CREAM

SERVES FOUR

The ridged pasta tubes of penne trap the nuggets of garlic, tomato, and pancetta in this sauce perfectly. Pancetta, in case you're not familiar with it, is an Italian cured bacon sold in many supermarkets and Italian specialty stores. If you can't find it, substitute pepper bacon. Feel free to omit the bacon for a vegetarian main course.

> 1 pound/500 g fresh penne or other ridged pasta tubes
> 1 teaspoon salt
> 1 teaspoon olive oil
> ¼ pound/120 g pancetta, diced
> 1 head garlic, roasted (see page 144)
> 3 cloves garlic, chopped
> 2 large tomatoes, diced
> ½ cup/120 mL/4 fl oz dry white wine
> 1½ cups/375 mL/12 fl oz heavy (double) cream
> ½ cup/90 g/3 ounces good-quality grated Parmesan cheese
> salt and freshly ground black pepper, to taste
> 1 tablespoon chopped fresh basil, or ½ tablespoon dried

Bring 8 cups/2 L/64 fl oz salted water to a boil in a large pot. Add the penne. Return the water to a boil and cook the pasta for 2 or 3 minutes, or until al dente. Drain the pasta, toss with the olive oil, and set aside.

In a very large sauté pan over high heat, cook the diced pancetta for 2 or 3 minutes, or until crisp. Remove the pancetta from the sauté pan and set it aside.

Squeeze the pulp from the head of roasted garlic. Add it and the chopped garlic to the pancetta oil in the pan and sauté until the mixture begins to give off its aroma, 2 or 3 minutes. Add the tomatoes and sauté for 1 to 2 minutes. Add the wine and cook for 3 or 4 minutes, or until about 2 tablespoons of the liquid remain. Add the cream and cook for 4 to 5 more minutes, or until the cream thickens. Add half the Parmesan cheese and season the mixture with salt and pepper. Add the pasta and pancetta, mix together, and cook just until the pasta is heated through.

Place the Penne with Garlic Cream on a platter and top with the remaining Parmesan and the chopped basil.

BAKED ZITI WITH THREE CHEESES

SERVES FOUR

Like the penne called for in the preceding recipe, ziti is a tube-shaped pasta, but a bit smaller than the penne. I tend to like tube-shaped pasta. I just love how the sauce gets trapped in the tubes and then explodes in your mouth. Kids usually love it, too.

      2 tomatoes, quartered
      1 yellow onion, quartered
      ¾ cup/120 mL/4 fl oz olive oil
      1 pound/500 g ziti or other pasta tubes
      3 cloves garlic, chopped
      2 shallots, chopped
      ⅓ pound/90 g mushrooms, sliced
      1 cup/250 mL/8 fl oz dry white wine
      2 cups/500 mL/16 fl oz heavy (double) cream
      3 ounces/90 g Gorgonzola cheese, crumbled
      2 ounces/60 g fontina cheese, grated
      2 ounces/60 g Parmesan cheese, grated
      salt and freshly ground black pepper, to taste

Preheat the oven to 425° F/210° C/gas mark 7.

Place the tomatoes and onion in a baking dish and toss with ½ cup/120 mL/4 fl oz of the olive oil. Roast until the tomatoes are blistered, about 25 minutes. Remove the tomatoes, set aside, and continue roasting the onion until tender, about 15 minutes more.

While the vegetables are roasting, bring 8 cups/2 L/64 fl oz salted water to a boil in a large pot. Add the ziti and boil until al dente, about 10 minutes. Drain and toss with 2 tablespoons of the olive oil. Set aside in a large bowl.

In a large saucepan over high temperature, heat the remaining olive oil. Add the garlic and shallots and sauté until they give off their aroma, 2 or 3 minutes. Add the mushrooms and sauté until tender, about 3 minutes. Add the wine and continue cooking over high heat until half the liquid remains, about 4 minutes. Add the cream and cook, stirring, until the mixture coats the back of a wooden spoon, about 5 minutes. Whisk in the cheeses just until blended. Set aside to cool.

When the onion has finished roasting, reduce the oven temperature to 350° F/175° C/gas mark 4. Grease a baking dish 9 × 11 inches/23 × 28 cm.

Roughly chop the onion and tomatoes and toss with the ziti. Place the ziti in the prepared baking dish. Pour the cooled sauce over the pasta and bake for 25 to 30 minutes, until golden brown.

Allow the mixture to stand for 2 or 3 minutes before serving the Baked Ziti family-style.

FETTUCINE WITH WILD MUSHROOMS
SERVES FOUR

This is a luxurious dish, so rich, layered with flavor and texture. Add a few dried mushrooms, if you'd like, to really pump up the flavor, but don't get carried away—they can be overpowering. Keep it luxurious with Champagne Fruit Compote for dessert.

1 pound/500 g fresh fettucine
1 tablespoon olive oil
2 shallots, chopped
3 cloves garlic, chopped
1 onion, julienned
1 pound/500 g assorted wild mushrooms (such as shiitake, chanterelles, morels), sliced
1 cup/250 mL/8 fl oz dry red wine
½ cup/120 mL/4 fl oz Vegetable Stock (see page 141)
2 tablespoons/30 g/1 ounce butter
1 tablespoon freshly ground black pepper
1 tablespoon chopped fresh savory, or ½ tablespoon dried
salt, to taste

Bring 8 cups/2 L/64 fl oz salted water to a boil in a large pot. Add the fettucine and boil until al dente, about 90 seconds. Drain and set aside.

In a large sauté pan over high temperature, heat the olive oil until very hot. Add the shallots, garlic, and onion and cook until they give off their aroma, 2 or 3 minutes. Add the mushrooms and sauté until the mushrooms are tender, about 4 minutes. Add the wine and continue cooking until half the liquid remains, about another 4 minutes. Add the stock and boil for 3 or 4 minutes more, until about three quarters of the liquid remains. Add the butter, black pepper, savory, and salt and mix well. Add the fettucine and toss well for a minute or two to reheat the pasta and blend it well with the sauce.

Serve the Fettucine with Wild Mushrooms immediately accompanied with a green salad.

SPICY VEGETABLE STIR-FRY

SERVES FOUR

The depth and dimension added by coconut milk and curry paste transforms the familiar vegetable stir-fry. This recipe is just a little bit spicy but, of course, you can always adjust the heat. Poached Pear Tart would round out your meal nicely.

2 tablespoons olive oil
1 medium eggplant (aubergine), diced
3 cloves garlic, chopped
2 shallots, chopped
1 red (Spanish) onion, julienned
1 zucchini (courgette), diced
1 yellow squash (or courgette), diced
2 red bell peppers (capsicums), diced
1 tomato, seeded and chopped
1 teaspoon curry paste
1 teaspoon fresh cilantro (coriander), chopped, or ½ teaspoon dried
¼ cup/60 mL/2 fl oz sake or dry white wine
¼ cup/60 mL/2 fl oz rice vinegar
¼ cup/60 mL/2 fl oz coconut milk
2 teaspoons chile paste
soy sauce, to taste

In a very large sauté pan or wok, heat the olive oil over high temperature until very hot. Add the eggplant and brown well. Add the garlic and shallots and sauté until they give off their aroma, about 2 or 3 minutes. Add the onion and sauté for 1 minute more. Add the zucchini, squash, and peppers and sauté for 2 or 3 minutes. Add the tomato and mix the vegetables together. Add the curry paste, cilantro, sake, rice vinegar, and coconut milk, stir to blend, and cook for 3 or 4 minutes, until about ½ cup/120 mL/6 fl oz liquid remains. Add the chile paste and season with soy sauce.

Serve the Spicy Vegetable Stir-Fry immediately over steamed basmati rice.

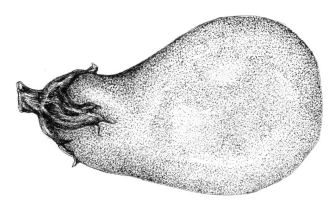

PESTO PIZZA

SERVES FOUR

Homemade pizza takes a bit of work, but it beats out take-away any day. The crust itself has a lot of flavor and can be used with a variety of toppings: tomato sauce, different vegetables or cheeses—goat cheese and Gorgonzola are both good with the pesto. Tomato Mussel Soup and this pizza would make a savory supper.

■ PIZZA DOUGH

1 tablespoon dry active yeast
1¼ cups/310 mL/10 fl oz warm water (under 110° F/55° C)
¼ teaspoon sugar
2 tablespoons olive oil, plus a little extra for greasing
2 teaspoons chopped fresh rosemary, or 1 teaspoon dried
¼ cup/50 g/1½ ounces grated Parmesan cheese
3 cups/450 g/1 pound all-purpose (plain) flour
1 teaspoon salt

■ PESTO

1 cup/120 g/4 ounces fresh basil leaves
3 cloves garlic, chopped
¼ cup/120 g/4 ounces pine nuts (kernels) or walnuts
¼ cup/60 mL/2 fl oz olive oil
salt, to taste

cornmeal (polenta/finely ground maize), for dusting
½ cup/60 g/2 ounces waterpacked or steamed fresh artichoke hearts
4 ounces/120 g mozzarella cheese, grated
¼ cup/50 g/1½ ounces grated Parmesan cheese
¼ cup/90 g/3 ounces Kalamata olives, chopped

Place the yeast, ¼ cup/60 mL/2 fl oz water, and sugar in a large mixing bowl. Stir and set aside until the yeast foams, about 10 minutes.

Transfer the mixture to the bowl of an electric mixer. Add the remaining water, olive oil, rosemary, and cheese. Using the dough hook, mix on low speed just to blend. Still on low speed, add the flour one sixth at a time. Add the salt and continue mixing until the dough is smooth and elastic, 3 or 4 minutes.

While the dough is mixing, flour your work surface and grease a large mixing bowl with some olive oil.

Remove the dough to the floured work surface and knead for a minute or two to form a smooth ball. Place the dough in the greased bowl, cover with a towel or plastic wrap (film), and set aside in a warm spot until it has doubled in bulk, about 1½ hours.

Meanwhile, prepare the pesto. In a food processor, puree the basil leaves, garlic, and nuts. With the motor running, gradually add the olive oil until thoroughly blended. Season with salt and set the pesto aside.

Preheat the oven and, if you have one, your pizza stone for 20 minutes at 450° F/230° C/gas mark 8 in the top third of the oven.

When the dough has doubled in bulk, turn it out onto a floured work surface. Roll it (or stretch it with your hands) into a circle 12 inches/30 cm in diameter and about ¼ inch/1 cm thick.

If you have a pizza paddle, lightly dust it with cornmeal. If you don't, grease a baking sheet and dust it with cornmeal. Place the circle of dough on top and spread it with pesto. Distribute the artichoke hearts, mozzarella, Parmesan, and olives evenly over all. Slide the pizza onto the stone; or set the baking sheet in the top third of the oven. Bake until the crust is golden brown and the cheese bubbling, 15 to 20 minutes.

Allow the Pesto Pizza to rest for a minute or two before slicing.

SIDE DISHES

- John's Sesame Noodles   *101*
- Rice Pilaf   *102*
- Soft Polenta with Roasted Herbs   *103*
- Caramelized-Onion Potato Gratin   *104*
- Herbed Oven-Roasted Fries   *105*
- Onion Potato Pancake   *106*
- Roasted Vegetables   *107*
- Lemon Pepper Asparagus   *108*
- Grilled Artichokes with Rosemary   *109*
- Marinated Broccoli   *110*

JOHN'S SESAME NOODLES
SERVES SIX

My own preference is to eat John's Sesame Noodles warm. In the restaurant, we often make an even bigger batch than usual for the kitchen and wait staff.

>½ pound/250 g dry Asian egg noodles
>2 tablespoons soy sauce
>2 cloves garlic, chopped
>1 teaspoon hot pepper flakes
>1 teaspoon sesame oil
>¼ cup/60 mL/2 fl oz vegetable oil

In a large stockpot over high heat, bring 2 quarts/4 L of water to a boil. Add the noodles and cook for 4 or 5 minutes, or until al dente. Drain the noodles into a serving bowl and set them aside.

In a small bowl, whisk together the soy sauce, garlic, hot pepper flakes, sesame oil, and vegetable oil until well blended and pour over the noodles.

Serve John's Sesame Noodles warm or at room temperature.

RICE PILAF
SERVES FOUR

Pilaf is a no-fail method of cooking rice, just as long as you follow a few simple steps: coat the rice with butter first and always bring the stock to a boil before you put the dish in the oven. It comes out perfect every time.

  2 teaspoons/10 g/⅓ ounce unsalted butter
  1 small onion, minced
  3 cloves garlic, chopped
  2 jalapeño peppers, seeded and chopped
  1 cup/220 g/7 ounces long-grain rice
  2 cups/500 mL/16 fl oz Chicken or Vegetable Stock (see page 141)
  ½ teaspoon ground cumin
  ½ teaspoon chopped fresh cilantro (coriander)

Preheat the oven to 350° F/175° C/gas mark 4.

In a medium casserole dish over high temperature, heat the butter until very hot. Add the onion and garlic and sauté until they begin to give off their aroma, 2 or 3 minutes. Add the chopped jalapeño and rice and toss to coat the rice with butter. Add the stock, cumin, and cilantro and heat just to a boil. Place the casserole in the oven, covered, and cook for 20 to 25 minutes, or until all the liquid has evaporated and the rice is tender.

Fluff the rice with a fork and serve immediately.

SOFT POLENTA WITH ROASTED HERBS

SERVES FOUR

More comfort food for the nineties. Soft Polenta is a dish that has the texture of cream of wheat or a soft porridge, but sure doesn't taste like either one of them. Roasting the herbs lends them an even fuller flavor, giving the dish its special savor.

1 teaspoon olive oil
2 cloves garlic, chopped
2 shallots, chopped
2 cups/500 mL/16 fl oz Chicken or Vegetable Stock (see page 141)
⅔ cup/55 g/2 ounces finely ground polenta (cornmeal/maize)
1 ounce/30 g soft, mild goat cheese
¼ cup/60 mL/2 fl oz heavy (double) cream
salt and freshly ground black pepper, to taste
2 teaspoons/10 g/⅓ ounce unsalted butter
1 tablespoon chopped fresh herbs (such as basil, thyme, rosemary)

In a large saucepan, heat olive oil over high temperature until very hot. Add the garlic and shallots and sauté until they begin to give off their aroma, 2 or 3 minutes. Add the stock and heat just to a boil. Gradually whisk in the polenta to avoid lumps from forming. Cook until the polenta is thick, 3 or 4 minutes. Add the cheese and cream and mix well. Season with salt and pepper and remove from the heat. Set aside.

In a small sauté pan over high heat, cook the butter until golden brown, 2 or 3 minutes. Add the herbs and immediately remove the pan from the heat. Stir the pan-roasted herbs into the polenta and serve straight away.

CARAMELIZED-ONION POTATO GRATIN

SERVES SIX

When you prepare this side dish, it's a good idea to use a nonstick pan—it makes removal and clean-up a lot easier. Caramelized-Onion Potato Gratin is particularly good with roast or grilled lamb.

5 medium potatoes, peeled
2 tablespoons olive oil
1 large onion, diced
1 cup/250 mL/8 fl oz heavy (double) cream
1 teaspoon minced fresh rosemary, or ½ teaspoon dried
salt and freshly ground black pepper, to taste
¾ cup/145 g/4 ounces grated fontina cheese
¼ cup/20 g/¾ ounce cured black olives, roughly chopped

Preheat the oven to 425° F/210° C/gas mark 7.

Slice the potatoes as thinly as you can, cover them with water, and set aside.

In a small sauté pan over high temperature, heat 1 tablespoon of the olive oil until smoking hot. Add the onion and cook until the onion has caramelized to dark brown, about 5 minutes. Set aside to cool.

In a small bowl, mix together the cream, rosemary, and salt and pepper. Set aside.

Drain the potatoes. In a large ovenproof pan, heat the remaining tablespoon of olive oil until very hot. Add enough potatoes to cover the bottom of the pan (about one third of the potatoes) and cook until they are browned.

Remove the pan from the heat and sprinkle about half the sautéed onion over the potatoes, then half the grated fontina and half the chopped olives. Drizzle with half the seasoned cream. Add a layer of uncooked potatoes, then the remaining onion, cheese, and olives. Drizzle with the remaining cream and top with a final layer of uncooked potatoes.

Place the pan in the oven and bake until the potatoes are fork-tender, 25 to 35 minutes. Set aside to cool for 5 minutes, then flip over onto a large plate.

Serve the Caramelized-Onion Potato Gratin warm.

HERBED OVEN-ROASTED FRIES

SERVES FOUR

Serve these potatoes with Beef with Arugula Pesto or any time you'd think of plain old baked potatoes.

    4 baking potatoes, scrubbed
    ¼ cup/60 mL/2 fl oz olive oil
    2 tablespoons chopped fresh herbs (such as rosemary, basil, thyme)
    2 teaspoons cracked black pepper
    kosher salt, to taste

Preheat the oven to 450° F/225° C/gas mark 5.

Cut the potatoes lengthwise into about 8 large wedges each. In a large bowl, toss them with the olive oil. Place in a roasting pan or on a baking sheet and roast for about 20 minutes. Sprinkle over the herbs and pepper and roast until the potatoes are golden brown and tender, 10 to 15 minutes more. Season with the kosher salt and serve the Herbed Oven-Roasted Fries immediately.

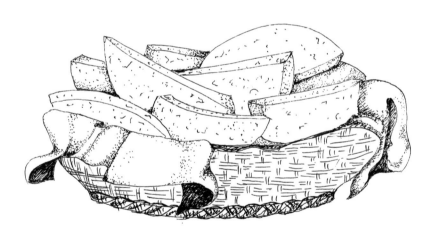

ONION POTATO PANCAKE

SERVES TWO

Caramelizing the onion gives an old favorite a new flavor dimension. This is a popular brunch item at our house.

    2 large baking potatoes
    2 tablespoons olive oil
    1 small onion, diced
    salt and freshly ground black pepper, to taste

Place the potatoes in a saucepan and cover them with water. Bring to a boil over high heat and cook until just tender, 15 to 25 minutes. Drain the potatoes and set aside until cool enough to handle.

Grate the potatoes into a bowl and set aside.

In a medium sauté pan over high temperature, heat 1 tablespoon of the olive oil until very hot. Add the onion and sauté until browned, 2 or 3 minutes. Add the grated potatoes and press to form a large pancake. Sauté until the bottom of the pancake is golden brown, 4 or 5 minutes. Remove with a spatula to a large flat plate. Heat the remaining olive oil in the pan. Return the pancake to the pan, uncooked side down, and sauté until golden brown on the bottom, 4 or 5 minutes more. Season the Onion Potato Pancake with salt and pepper and serve straight away.

ROASTED VEGETABLES
SERVES FOUR

You'll maybe have guessed by now that I like roasting vegetables. Garlic, shallots, whatever—it brings out their natural sugars and deepens their flavors. These are delicious just by themselves or as an accompaniment.

    3 potatoes
    2 carrots
    1 large onion
    1 sweet potato
    1 small celeriac, peeled
    1 tablespoon olive oil
    5 cloves garlic, peeled
    1 tablespoon chopped fresh thyme, or ½ tablespoon dried
    salt and freshly ground black pepper, to taste

Preheat the oven to 425° F/210° C/gas mark 7.

Cut the potatoes, carrots, onion, sweet potato, and celeriac into dice ¼ inch/0.5 cm. Set aside.

Place the olive oil in a roasting pan and put it in the oven until the oil is smoking hot. Remove the pan from the oven and add all the prepared vegetables and the garlic. Cook until the vegetables are tender and caramelized golden brown, about 15 minutes. Stir infrequently so the vegetables have a chance to brown.

Just before serving the Roasted Vegetables, add the thyme and season with salt and pepper.

LEMON PEPPER ASPARAGUS

SERVES FOUR

When asparagus first arrives in the market, and it's affordable, it means spring can't be far away. Which is why I love it. Serve these zesty spears with some spring lamb in celebration of the new season.

> 1 pound/500 g asparagus spears, trimmed
> ½ cup/120 g/4 ounces unsalted butter
> 3 cloves garlic, chopped
> 1 shallot, chopped
> 1 teaspoon lemon zest
> 1 tablespoon freshly cracked black pepper
> juice of 1 lemon
> salt, to taste

Bring 8 cups/2 L/64 fl oz salted water to a boil in a large pot. Add the asparagus spears and boil until tender, about 4 minutes. Drain and set aside in a large bowl.

In a large sauté pan over high temperature, heat the butter until bubbling. Add the garlic and shallot and cook for about 1 minute, taking care not to burn the garlic. Add the zest and pepper and cook until the butter begins to brown, about 2 minutes. Add the lemon juice and salt. Remove from the heat and toss with the asparagus.

Serve the Lemon Pepper Asparagus immediately.

GRILLED ARTICHOKES WITH ROSEMARY

SERVES FOUR

The artichokes in this dish are already cooked before you put them on the grill or barbecue to give them a delicious smoky flavor, so be sure not to overgrill them. These are good with other simply grilled vegetables or meats or as an appetizer all by themselves.

4 (globe) artichokes
½ cup/120 mL/4 fl oz balsamic vinegar
4 cloves garlic, chopped
2 shallots, chopped
2 teaspoons chopped fresh rosemary, or 1 teaspoon dried
1 cup/250 mL/8 fl oz olive oil
2 teaspoons cracked black pepper
salt, to taste.

Trim the stems from the artichokes and about ½ inch/5 cm from the tops.

Bring 1 gallon/4 L salted water to a boil in a large pot. Add the trimmed artichokes and cook until tender, 15 to 20 minutes. Drain and set aside until cool enough to handle. Cut each artichoke in half and remove the hairy choke. Set aside in a large nonreactive bowl.

In a bowl, whisk together the vinegar, garlic, shallots, rosemary, olive oil, pepper, and salt. Pour over the artichoke halves and toss together well. Set aside to marinate for 30 minutes while you prepare the coals.

Using tongs, place the artichokes on the grill (barbecue) and cook for 3 or 4 minutes per side, until the vegetables are marked by the grill.

Drizzle the Grilled Artichokes with the remaining marinade and serve warm.

MARINATED BROCCOLI

SERVES FOUR

I like to use Chinese broccoli for this dish with its Asian flavors, but it's not the end of the world if you can't find it. Marinated Broccoli is particularly nice with grilled fish or chicken.

> 1 bunch broccoli (about 1½ pounds/750 g)
> 2 tablespoons oyster sauce
> 1 clove garlic, chopped
> juice of 1 lime
> 1 tablespoon olive oil
> 1 tablespoon sesame oil

Bring 12 cups/3 L/96 fl oz water to a boil in a large pot. Add the broccoli and boil until crisp-tender, about 5 minutes. Drain the broccoli and immediately plunge it into a bowl of ice water for 5 minutes.

Meanwhile, prepare the marinade by whisking together the oyster sauce, garlic, lime juice, and olive and sesame oils in a small bowl.

Drain the broccoli and place it in a large nonreactive bowl. Pour over the marinade and toss well.

Set the Marinated Broccoli aside for 2 or 3 hours to allow the flavors to blend before serving.

DESSERTS

■ Strawberry Peach Tart   *113*

■ Raspberry Lemon Curd Tart   *114*

■ Free-Form Apple Tart   *115*

■ Chocolate Praline Tart   *116*

■ Poached Pear Tart   *117*

■ Ricotta Raspberry Tart   *118*

■ Strawberry Streusel   *119*

■ Triple Chocolate Hazelnut Torte   *120*

■ Plum Spice Cake   *121*

■ Chocolate Almond Cheesecake   *122*

■ White Chocolate Cheesecake   *123*

■ Ginger Peach Upside-Down Cake   *124*

■ Blackberry Lemon Soufflés with Lemon Sauce   *125*

■ Apple Almond Bread Pudding   *126*

■ Berry Trifles   *127*

■ Orange Crème Brûlée   *128*

■ Cinnamon Rum Flan   *129*

■ Mocha Pots de Crème   *130*

■ Pumpkin Crème Brûlée   *131*

■ Champagne Fruit Compote   *132*

■ Coffee Granita   *133*

■ Raspberry Port Ice Cream   *134*

■ Caprial's Jammers   *135*

■ Chocolate Pecan Shortbread   *136*

STRAWBERRY PEACH TART

SERVES EIGHT TO TWELVE

This tart depends on the flavor of the fruit and berries, so make sure they're perfectly ripe. The Chocolate Crust (see page 116) is also wonderful in this dessert.

■ ALMOND CRUST

½ cup/60 g/2 ounces blanched almonds

1½ cups/250 g/8 ounces all-purpose (plain) flour

½ cup/90 g/3 ounces confectioners' (icing) sugar

½ teaspoon ground cinnamon

1 teaspoon vanilla extract

1 teaspoon salt

1 cup/250 g/8 ounces unsalted butter

■ FILLING

1½ cups/90 g/3 ounces strawberries, stemmed and quartered

4 peaches, peeled and sliced

¾ cup/185 g/6 ounces granulated sugar

zest of 1 orange

¼ teaspoon ground nutmeg

¼ teaspoon ground ginger

Preheat the oven to 350° F/175° C/gas mark 4.

For the crust, grind the almonds in a food processor. Place the flour, sugar, cinnamon, vanilla, and salt in the food processor. Turn the machine on and slowly add the butter, 2 tablespoons/30 g/1 ounce at a time. Process until the dough forms a ball on top of the blades.

Press the dough into a 12-inch/30-cm tart pan with a removable bottom. Prebake for 10 minutes, or until the crust is light brown. Set aside to cool.

Leave the oven on while you prepare the filling.

In a medium bowl, mix the prepared strawberries and peaches. Add the sugar, orange zest, nutmeg, and ginger and toss together well. Spoon the mixture evenly into the crust. Bake until the crust is golden brown and the fruit bubbling, 20 to 30 minutes.

Serve the tart warm, alone or accompanied by vanilla ice cream.

RASPBERRY LEMON CURD TART

SERVES EIGHT TO TWELVE

When I make this tart in the summer, I top the whole thing with fresh raspberries and a dusting of confectioners', or icing, sugar. When I make it in winter, it's so bright and cheerful it reminds me of the sunshine, which we don't see much of here that time of year.

■ SWEET CRUST
2 cups/315 g/10 ounces all-purpose (plain) flour
½ cup/90 g/3 ounces confectioners' (icing) sugar
½ teaspoon salt
½ teaspoon vanilla extract
1 cup/250 g/8 ounces unsalted butter

■ FILLING
1 egg
4 egg yolks
1¼ cups/315 g/10 ounces granulated sugar
½ cup/120 mL/4 fl oz lemon juice
1 tablespoon lemon zest
pinch salt
½ cup/120 g/4 ounces unsalted butter
⅓ cup/80 mL/3 fl oz raspberry jam

Preheat the oven to 350° F/175° C/gas mark 4.

To make the crust, place the flour, confectioners' sugar, salt, and vanilla in a food processor. Turn the machine on and add the butter, 2 tablespoons/30 g/1 ounce at a time. Process until a ball forms on top of the blades.

Press the dough into a 12-inch/30-cm tart pan with a removable bottom. Bake the crust for 10 minutes, or until it turns light brown. Set the crust aside for 15 minutes to cool.

For the filling, whisk together the egg, egg yolks, and granulated sugar in a medium bowl until the eggs are foamy. Place the lemon juice, zest, pinch of salt, and the butter in a medium stainless steel bowl. Place the bowl over a pot of barely simmering water and mix until the butter has melted. Add the egg mixture to the lemon mixture and cook over medium heat until the mixture is very thick and heavily coats the back of a spoon, 15 to 20 minutes. Set the lemon curd aside to cool slightly.

Spread the raspberry jam over the bottom of the prebaked crust. Pour the lemon curd over the jam and chill the tart in the refrigerator for 3 to 4 hours.

Raspberry Lemon Curd Tart is great served with Berry Orange Sauce (see page 146).

FREE-FORM APPLE TART
SERVES EIGHT TO TWELVE

Although I call this apple tart "free-form," I do put it in a pan, so it's not completely lacking in shape. "Rustic" is maybe a better description—so is "comforting and easy to clean up and carry."

■ SHORTENING CRUST
1¼ cups/200 g/6 ounces all-purpose (plain) flour
½ cup/120 g/4 ounces vegetable shortening (white vegetable fat)
½ teaspoon salt
6 tablespoons water

■ FILLING
5 tart apples, preferably Granny Smith, peeled and sliced
½ cup/120 g/4 ounces sugar
1 teaspoon ground cinnamon
½ teaspoon ground allspice
pinch ground cloves
pinch ground nutmeg
1 teaspoon vanilla extract
1 tablespoon/15 g/½ ounce unsalted butter, cut in small pieces

■ TOPPING
¼ cup/60 g/2 ounces unsalted butter, softened
⅓ cup/90 g/3 ounces sugar
¼ cup/45 g/1½ ounces all-purpose (plain) flour

To make the crust, place the flour, shortening, and salt in a medium bowl. Mix the shortening with your fingers until it is well distributed and the mixture resembles coarse meal. Drizzle in the water while mixing the dough with a fork. Mix the dough just until it begins to come together. Wrap in plastic wrap (film) and set aside for at least 15 minutes.

Preheat the oven to 425° F/210° C/gas mark 7.

On a floured board, roll the dough out to a disc 14 inches/35 cm diameter. Then fold the dough gently into quarters, and then out into a 12-inch/30-cm tart pan with a removable bottom. Set aside.

To make the filling, place the apples, sugar, cinnamon, allspice, cloves, nutmeg, and vanilla in a medium bowl and mix well. Toss in the small pieces of butter. Spread the apples over the bottom of the prepared crust and set aside.

To prepare the topping, in a small bowl mix together the softened butter, sugar, and flour to form a crumbly dough. Spread the topping evenly over the apples. Fold the overhanging dough over the topping all the way around the tart.

Bake the tart for 15 minutes, then reduce the heat to 350° F/175° C/gas mark 4. Bake for 20 more minutes, or until the tart is golden brown.

Allow the tart to cool slightly and serve, still warm, with vanilla ice cream.

CHOCOLATE PRALINE TART

SERVES EIGHT TO TWELVE

Here's another of John's recipes and just one of the reasons I married him. Customers at the restaurant say it's like a little slice of heaven.

■ CHOCOLATE CRUST
1½ cups/250 g/8 ounces all-purpose (plain) flour
½ cup/90 g/3 ounces cocoa powder
¾ cup/145 g/4 ounces confectioners' (icing) sugar
1 teaspoon vanilla extract
1 teaspoon salt
1 cup/250 g/8 ounces unsalted butter

■ FILLING
1⅔ cups/420 g/13 ounces unsalted butter
1½ cups/280 g/9 ounces light or dark brown sugar
¼ cup/60 g/2 ounces granulated sugar
⅔ cup/250 g/8 fl oz (clear) honey
3 cups/360 g/12 ounces pecan halves
⅓ cup/80 mL/3 fl oz heavy (double) cream

Preheat the oven to 350° F/175° C/gas mark 4.

For the crust, place the flour, cocoa, confectioners' sugar, vanilla, and salt in a food processor. Turn the machine on and gradually add the butter, 2 tablespoons/30 g/1 ounce at a time. Process until the dough forms a ball on top of the blades. Press the dough into a 12-inch/30-cm tart pan with a removable bottom. Prebake for 10 minutes, or until light brown. Set aside to cool.

Leave the oven on while you prepare the filling.

In a large saucepan, bring the butter, brown and granulated sugars, and honey to a boil over medium-high heat. Boil for 3 minutes. Add the pecans and cream and return to a boil. Immediately pour the mixture into the cooled crust. Bake for about 20 minutes, or until the center of the mixture is bubbling. Let the tart cool to room temperature, or about 2 hours.

POACHED PEAR TART
SERVES EIGHT TO TWELVE

You won't believe how good your kitchen will smell when you cook this very delicate tart! Leave the pears to cool in the poaching liquid to give them lots of color and to keep that wonderful aroma around for a little while longer. (These poached pears, by the way, also make a simple delicious dessert just as they are.)

■ CINNAMON CRUST

2 cups/315 g/10 ounces all-purpose (plain) flour
½ cup/90 g/3 ounces confectioners' (icing) sugar
1 teaspoon vanilla extract
1 cup/250 g/8 ounces unsalted butter
½ teaspoon salt
½ teaspoon ground cinnamon

■ FILLING

5 pears
2 cups/500 mL/16 fl oz red wine
1 cup/250 g/8 ounces granulated sugar
¾ cup/180 mL/6 fl oz heavy (double) cream
½ cup/155 g/5 ounces almond paste
3 eggs
2 teaspoons almond extract

Preheat the oven to 350° F/175° C/gas mark 4.

To make the crust, place the flour, confectioners' sugar, and vanilla extract in a food processor. Turn the machine on and slowly add the butter, 2 tablespoons/30 g/1 ounce at a time. Add the salt and cinnamon and process until the dough forms a ball on top of the blades.

Press the dough into a 12-inch/30-cm tart pan with a removable bottom. Prebake the crust about 10 minutes, or until light brown. Set aside to cool.

Leave the oven on while you prepare the rest of the tart.

Peel, core, and halve the pears. In a medium saucepan over high heat, bring the wine and half of the granulated sugar just to a boil. Add the pears and cook over medium heat until the pears are fork-tender, 10 to 15 minutes. Set aside to let the pears cool in the wine mixture.

Slice the pears lengthwise and arrange them in the crust in slightly overlapping concentric circles. Set aside. Freeze the wine mixture for another use or discard it.

Blend the cream, almond paste, and remaining granulated sugar in the food processor until smooth. Add the eggs and almond extract and mix well. Pour the mixture slowly over the pears. Bake the tart for 25 to 30 minutes, or until a tester inserted into the center of the custard comes out clean.

Serve warm or at room temperature.

RICOTTA RASPBERRY TART

SERVES EIGHT TO TWELVE

Ricotta Raspberry Tart is an excellent brunch dessert. Either fresh or frozen berries can be used—frozen will make the tart a bit more juicy.

> 2 cups/250 g/8 ounces ricotta cheese
> zest of 1 orange
> 4 eggs
> ½ cup/120 g/4 ounces granulated sugar
> 4 cups/250 g/8 ounces raspberries (2 pints)
> ¾ cup/185 g/6 ounces unsalted butter
> ½ cup/90 g/3 ounces confectioners' (icing) sugar
> 1½ cups/250 g/8 ounces all-purpose (plain) flour
> ½ cup/60 g/2 ounces toasted almonds
> ½ teaspoon almond extract
> ½ teaspoon salt

Preheat the oven to 350° F/175° C/gas mark 4. Grease well a 12-inch/30-cm springform pan.

In a large bowl, mix together the ricotta and orange zest. Lightly beat 3 of the eggs and add them and the granulated sugar to the ricotta. Mix well. Pour the mixture into the prepared pan and top with the raspberries. Set aside.

In a medium bowl, mix together well the butter and confectioners' sugar. Add the remaining egg and mix again. Add the flour, almonds, almond extract, and salt and mix well.

Crumble this topping mixture over the raspberries and bake for 35 to 45 minutes, or until a tester inserted in the center of the cheese custard comes out clean.

Allow the tart to cool completely before chilling in the refrigerator for an hour or 2. Serve chilled.

STRAWBERRY STREUSEL

SERVES EIGHT TO TWELVE

Crispy-topped strawberry pie is an elegant but simple way to put together a dessert for those surprise guests.

> 4 cups/250 g/8 ounces strawberries (2 pints)
> 1 recipe Shortening Crust (see page 115)
> 1 cup/250 g/8 ounces sugar
> zest of 1 orange
> 1 teaspoon cornstarch (cornflour powder)
> 4 tablespoons/60 g/2 ounces unsalted butter
> 3 tablespoons all-purpose (plain) flour
> pinch ground nutmeg
> pinch ground ginger

Preheat the oven to 350° F/175° C/gas mark 4. Grease well a 12-inch/30-cm tart pan with a removable bottom.

Stem, wash, and drain the strawberries.

On a floured board, roll the pie dough out to a disc ⅛ inch/3 mm thick. Ease into the prepared pan and prebake for 10 minutes, or until light brown.

In a large bowl, toss the strawberries with three quarters of the sugar, orange zest, and cornstarch. In another bowl, mix together the butter, the remaining sugar, flour, nutmeg, and ginger to a coarse meal.

Pour the strawberry mixture into the prebaked crust and crumble the butter mixture over the top. Bake until golden brown, 30 to 45 minutes.

Serve warm or at room temperature.

TRIPLE CHOCOLATE HAZELNUT TORTE

SERVES EIGHT TO TWELVE

This is the kind of multilayered confection you look at in the bakery and wish you could make at home. Well, you can! The bottom layer of dense chocolate hazelnut cake can be made ahead and frozen for later use, if you wish. Next comes a film of white chocolate, then a layer of smooth mousse. The ultimate in chocolate desserts!

> 10 ounces/300 g bittersweet (plain) chocolate
> ½ cup/120 g/4 ounces unsalted butter
> ¼ cup/60 g/2 ounces sugar
> 3 eggs, lightly beaten
> 1 cup/155 g/5 ounces unsweetened cocoa powder
> 1 cup/120 g/4 ounces ground hazelnuts
> ¼ cup/60 mL/2 fl oz hazelnut liqueur
> 4 ounces/120 g white chocolate
> 2¼ cups/560 mL/18 fl oz heavy (double) cream

Preheat the oven to 350° F/175° C/gas mark 4. Line a 9-inch/23-cm springform pan with aluminum foil.

Place 4 ounces/120 g of the bittersweet chocolate and the butter in a medium stainless steel bowl. Place the bowl over a pot of barely simmering water, making sure that the bottom doesn't touch the water, and heat until the chocolate and butter are melted.

Remove the bowl from the heat and mix in the sugar. Add the beaten eggs and mix thoroughly. Add the cocoa powder, nuts, and liqueur. Pour the mixture into the prepared pan. Bake for 15 to 20 minutes, or until a tester inserted in the center comes out clean. Set the cake aside to cool and then invert it onto a plate.

Place the white chocolate and ¼ cup/60 mL/2 fl oz of the heavy cream in a medium stainless steel bowl and place the bowl over the simmering water in the pot until the white chocolate has melted. Remove the bowl from the heat. Set the white chocolate aside to cool and thicken.

Pour the white chocolate over the cooled cake and spread it to cover the top and sides. Set aside in the refrigerator.

Melt the remaining bittersweet chocolate in a stainless steel bowl over the pot of simmering water. Remove the bowl from the heat and set it aside.

In an electric mixer on high speed, whip the remaining cream until it holds soft peaks. Fold about one third of the whipped cream into the melted bittersweet chocolate. Gently fold in the remaining whipped cream and pour the mixture over the cake, spreading it over the top and sides. Refrigerate the torte for at least 2 hours, or overnight.

Serve the Triple Chocolate Hazelnut Torte chilled with whipped cream.

opposite: Free-Form Apple Tart, page 115

PLUM SPICE CAKE

SERVES EIGHT TO TEN

It's the oil in this cake that makes it so moist. But it's not just the moistness that's so good: when this is baking, your kitchen will smell *so* incredible.

> 1 pound/500 g fresh plums
> 3 cups/470 g/15 ounces all-purpose (plain) flour
> 2 cups/500 g/16 ounces sugar
> 1 cup/250 mL/8 fl oz vegetable oil
> 3 eggs
> ½ teaspoon baking soda (bicarbonate of soda)
> 2 teaspoons ground cinnamon
> ½ teaspoon ground allspice
> ½ teaspoon ground nutmeg
> ½ teaspoon ground ginger
> ¼ teaspoon ground cloves
> 1 teaspoon vanilla extract
> 1 teaspoon almond extract
> ¼ teaspoon salt

Preheat the oven to 350° F/175° C/gas mark 4. Line a 9-inch/23-cm springform pan with aluminum foil.

Pit and halve the plums and place them, cut sides up, in the bottom of the pan. Set aside.

In an electric mixer, blend the flour, sugar, and oil on low speed until the flour is evenly moistened. Add the eggs and blend thoroughly.

In a small bowl, mix together the baking soda, cinnamon, allspice, nutmeg, ginger, and cloves. Add the spice mixture to the batter in the mixer and blend well. Scrape the sides and bottom of the bowl. Add the vanilla and almond extracts and the salt and mix again.

Pour the batter slowly over the plums. Bake the cake for 50 to 60 minutes, or until a tester inserted in the center comes out clean. Set aside to cool for 15 minutes before inverting onto a serving plate..

Serve the Plum Spice Cake warm with softly whipped cream.

opposite: Ricotta Raspberry Tart, page 118

CHOCOLATE ALMOND CHEESECAKE
SERVES EIGHT TO TWELVE

The last word in decadence. Hazelnuts, pecans, or your other favorite nut can be used instead of almonds in the crust. I've also been known to chop up 2 ounces of bittersweet chocolate —that's about 60 g—to add to the filling. Now maybe *that's* the last word in decadence!

■ TOASTED ALMOND CRUST
1½ cups/185 g/6 ounces toasted almonds
½ cup/120 g/4 ounces sugar
2 tablespoons/30 g/1 ounce unsalted butter, melted
½ teaspoon almond extract

■ FILLING
2 pounds/1 kg cream cheese
1½ cups/375 g/12 ounces sugar
4 eggs
5 ounces/155 g bittersweet (plain) chocolate, melted
½ teaspoon vanilla extract

In a food processor, blend the almonds and sugar to a coarse meal. Add the butter and almond extract and process until fully blended. Press the mixture into the bottom of a 9-inch/23-cm springform pan, bringing it up the sides to a height of ¼ inch/0.5 cm. Chill for 30 minutes.

Preheat the oven to 350° F/175° C/gas mark 4.

To prepare the filling, cut the cream cheese into 8 or 10 pieces and place in a mixer. Scraping the sides and bottom of the bowl frequently, blend until smooth. Add the sugar and mix thoroughly. Add the eggs one at a time, mixing well after each addition. When the eggs are fully incorporated, drizzle in the chocolate, mixing to blend. Turn off the machine and scrape the bottom and sides down well.

With the machine back on, add the vanilla and blend. Pour the mixture into the crust. Bake for 50 to 60 minutes, or until a tester inserted in the center comes out clean. Let the cheesecake cool and refrigerate for at least 4 hours.

Serve with whipped cream.

WHITE CHOCOLATE CHEESECAKE
SERVES EIGHT TO TWELVE

White Chocolate Cheesecake is made without a crust, but not without lots of flavor. Actually, it's also made without chocolate, because white chocolate isn't really chocolate at all: it's cocoa butter, milk, sugar, and vanilla. Sometimes it's difficult to work with, so I recommend you put it over very low heat on the stove only until it begins to melt and then just let it finish melting from the heat of the water bath.

> 2 pounds/1 kg cream cheese
> 1½ cups/375 g/12 ounces sugar
> 4 eggs
> 5 ounces/155 g white chocolate, melted
> zest of one lemon
> juice of one lemon
> ½ teaspoon vanilla extract

Preheat the oven to 350° F/175° C/gas mark 4. Grease well a 9-inch/23-cm springform pan and line it with aluminum foil.

In an electric mixer, blend the cream cheese on medium speed until smooth. Scrape the sides and bottom well. Add the sugar and blend. Add the eggs one at a time, mixing after each addition. With the motor running, drizzle in the white chocolate. Scrape the sides and bottom again and mix well.

Add the lemon zest and juice and the vanilla. Mix again. Scrape the sides and bottom and blend again.

Pour into the prepared pan and bake for about 1 hour, or until a tester inserted in the center of the cheesecake comes out clean. Set aside for 10 to 15 minutes before refrigerating. Chill for at least 4 hours before serving.

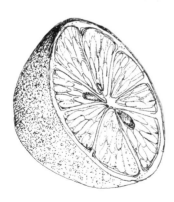

GINGER PEACH UPSIDE-DOWN CAKE
SERVES EIGHT TO TWELVE

Crystalized ginger is a special addition to many desserts. It brings this classic upside-down cake into the nineties. Be sure to serve it warm, though, and pass a bowl of softly whipped cream.

4 large peaches
¾ cup/60 g/2 ounces unsalted butter
½ cup/90 g/3 ounces brown sugar
2 large slices fresh ginger
¾ cup/185 g/6 ounces granulated sugar
3 egg yolks
½ cup/120 mL/4 fl oz sour cream (or crème fraîche)
1½ cups/250 g/8 ounces all-purpose (plain) flour
¾ teaspoon baking powder
¼ teaspoon baking soda (bicarbonate of soda)
1 teaspoon vanilla extract
1 tablespoon ground ginger

Preheat the oven to 350° F/175° C/gas mark 4. Grease an 8-inch/20-cm cake pan well.

Peel and thinly slice the peaches. Arrange them in the bottom of the prepared pan and set aside.

In a saucepan over medium temperature, heat to a boil one third of the butter, the brown sugar, and slices of ginger. Boil the mixture for 1 minute, then remove the slices of ginger. Pour the butter mixture gently over the peaches and set aside.

In a mixer, blend the remaining butter and granulated sugar until smooth and creamy. Add the egg yolks one at a time, mixing well after each one. Add the sour cream and mix well. Add the flour, baking powder and soda, vanilla, and ground ginger. Mix until the batter is smooth. Pour the batter over the peaches and bake for 40 to 50 minutes, or until the cake springs back when touched.

Let the cake cool slightly, then invert it onto a plate.

Serve warm with softly whipped cream.

BLACKBERRY LEMON SOUFFLÉS
WITH LEMON SAUCE
SERVES FOUR

I know, I know, soufflés are *scary*, but this recipe is so simple you can do it! Just think how spectacular serving a soufflé to your guests would be. I've also made this with other berries and fruits, so once you've had your first great success, you need never look back.

■ LEMON SAUCE
½ cup/120 mL/4 fl oz lemon juice
1½ cups/375 g/12 ounces granulated sugar
1 tablespoon/15 g/½ ounce butter
1 egg
3 egg yolks

■ SOUFFLÉS
4 cups/250 g/8 ounces blackberries (2 pints)
1 cup/250 g/8 ounces granulated sugar, plus a little extra for dusting
zest of 1 lemon
pinch ground ginger
pinch ground cinnamon
8 egg whites
confectioners' (icing) sugar, for dusting

To make the Lemon Sauce, place the lemon juice, the 1½ cups/375 g/12 ounces sugar, butter, egg, and egg yolks in a medium stainless steel bowl. Place the bowl over a pot of barely simmering water. Cook slowly, stirring constantly, until the mixture thickens enough to coat the back of a spoon, about 5 or 6 minutes. Remove from the heat and set aside to cool.

Preheat the oven to 400° F/200° C/gas mark 6. Butter the bottom and sides of 4 custard cups (6 fl oz/180 mL) and dust the sides with granulated sugar.

To make the soufflés, place the berries and three quarters of the sugar in a large saucepan over high heat. Bring the mixture to a boil and cook until the sugar dissolves, about 2 or 3 minutes. Cook an additional 3 to 5 minutes until the mixture thickens. Remove the mixture from the heat and strain through a fine sieve into a large bowl. Add the lemon zest, ginger, and cinnamon and mix well.

Place the egg whites in an electric mixer and process on high speed just until soft peaks begin to form. Sprinkle in the remaining granulated sugar, about 1 tablespoon at a time. Whip until the egg whites are glossy and soft, but not stiff.

Gently fold the egg whites into the blackberry mixture just until mixed (streaks are fine). Pour the mixture into the custard cups, smoothing the top of each one. Bake until the soufflés are puffed and golden, 20 to 25 minutes.

Remove from the oven and dust with confectioners' sugar.

Serve the Blackberry Lemon Soufflés immediately, with a pitcher of the Lemon Sauce passed around.

APPLE ALMOND BREAD PUDDING

SERVES EIGHT TO TWELVE

I started making this recipe years ago and it's still a restaurant favorite. The crunch of the caramelized topping contrasts nicely with the soft pudding below.

1 bagette (French loaf), diced
2 tart apples, preferably Granny Smith, sliced
1½ cups/185 g/6 ounces almonds, sliced
3 cups/750 mL/24 fl oz half-and-half (half milk, half cream)
¾ cup/185 g/6 ounces sugar
5 eggs
½ cup/155 g/5 ounces almond paste
1 teaspoon almond extract
1 teaspoon ground cinnamon
½ teaspoon ground nutmeg
½ teaspoon ground allspice

Line a 9-inch/23-cm springform pan with aluminum foil.

Place the diced bread in the pan. Add the sliced apples and almonds and, using your hands, mix well. Set aside.

In a medium bowl, mix together the half-and-half, sugar, and eggs. Add the almond paste, almond extract, cinnamon, nutmeg, and allspice and mix thoroughly until smooth. Pour over the bread mixture and stir to coat all the bread. Set aside for 20 minutes to allow the custard to soak into the bread.

Preheat the oven to 350° F/175° C/gas mark 4.

Stir the mixture again, then bake it for 45 minutes, or until the custard is set.

Serve the Apple Almond Bread Pudding warm.

BERRY TRIFLES

SERVES SIX

I can't think of a better way to use leftover cake and berries. You can even get away with using less-than-sweet berries if you sprinkle them with a couple tablespoons of sugar and let them sit for ten or fifteen minutes. I actually think these taste better made ahead of time; just don't add the cream until you're ready to serve.

> 12 slices Pound Cake (see page 146)
> ⅓ cup/80 mL/3 fl oz Grand Marnier or other orange liqueur
> 3 cups/185 g/6 ounces strawberries (1½ pints)
> 3 cups/185 g/6 ounces raspberries (1½ pints)
> 3 cups/185 g/6 ounces blackberries (1½ pints)
> 2 cups/250 mL/16 fl oz mascarpone cheese
> ⅓ cup/80 mL/3 fl oz whipping cream
> 1 tablespoon sugar
> sprigs of mint, for garnish

Line a baking sheet with plastic wrap (film). Place the poundcake slices on it and sprinkle with the Grand Marnier. Set aside for 5 minutes so the cake can soak up the liqueur.

Slice the strawberries and place them in a medium bowl. Add the raspberries and blackberries and toss together well.

Into the bottoms of 6 large wine glasses, crumble the soaked pound cake to a depth of about ½ inch/1 cm. Top each portion with about 3 or 4 tablespoons of the mixed berries, then about 2 tablespoons of the mascarpone. Distribute half the remaining pound cake among the glasses, then all but 3 tablespoons or so of the remaining berries. Spoon on the remaining mascarpone, then a final layer of pound cake.

In a bowl, whip the cream until it begins to thicken. Add the sugar and whip until soft peaks form. Top each of the Berry Trifles with the whipped cream and a few berries. Chill well.

Just before serving, garnish with sprigs of mint.

ORANGE CRÈME BRÛLÉE

SERVES FOUR

Crème brûlée is often baked in the oven, but then the consistency is more like that of a crème caramel. I cook mine on top of the stove and the result is so much more creamy and delicious. Be sure to add the orange juice concentrate right at the end so the crème doesn't curdle.

> 2 cups/500 mL/16 fl oz half-and-half (half milk, half cream)
> 5 egg yolks
> 1½ cups/375 g/12 ounces sugar
> 1 vanilla bean, split
> zest of 1 orange
> 1 tablespoon orange juice concentrate

In a heavy-bottomed saucepan over medium temperature, heat the half-and-half just to a boil and set aside.

Place the egg yolks and ⅓ cup/90 g/3 ounces sugar in a medium stainless steel bowl. Place the bowl over a pot of barely simmering water and whisk the mixture until a ribbon forms when you lift the whisk. Add the half-and-half and the vanilla bean and mix well. Add the zest and cook the mixture over the water bath, whisking constantly, until it reaches the consistency of softly whipped cream, 40 or 50 minutes.

Remove from the heat and whisk in the orange juice. Pour into 4 custard cups (8 fl oz/ 250 mL) and allow to cool for at least 4 hours, or overnight.

Just before serving, sprinkle the chilled creams with the remaining sugar. Place under a high broiler (grill) until the sugar turns golden brown, 2 or 3 minutes. (In my restaurant kitchen, I use a propane torch to brown the sugar!)

Serve immediately.

CINNAMON RUM FLAN

SERVES SIX

Here's a grown-up version of a childhood favorite. This creamy custard has the very adult addition of rum. By the way, don't be alarmed: the cinnamon is meant to float to the top.

1¼ cups/300 g/10 ounces sugar
⅓ cup/80 mL/3 fl oz water
2 cups/500 mL/16 fl oz half-and-half (half milk, half cream)
3 whole eggs
3 egg yolks
¼ cup/60 mL/2 fl oz dark rum
2 teaspoons ground cinnamon
½ teaspoon vanilla extract

Place ¾ cup/185 g/6 ounces of the sugar and the water in a medium sauté pan. Do not stir—allow the water to moisten the sugar. Over high heat, cook the sugar mixture, without stirring it, until it starts to brown. Stir to even the color to nut brown. Remove from the heat. Divide the sugar mixture among 6 custard cups (8 fl oz/250 mL) and set them aside to allow the sugar to set.

Preheat the oven to 350° F/175° C/gas mark 4.

Place the half-and-half in a large bowl and whisk in the eggs and egg yolks. Add the remaining sugar, rum, cinnamon, and vanilla and mix well. Pour the egg mixture onto the hardened sugar, dividing it equally among the cups. Place the cups in a baking dish. Pour enough water into the baking dish to come halfway up the sides of the cups.

Place the baking dish in the oven and bake for 50 to 60 minutes, or until a tester inserted in the center of a custard comes out clean. Refrigerate the flan for at least 4 hours, or overnight.

Run a knife around the edges of each Cinnamon Rum Flan and invert them onto individual plates. Serve immediately, still cold.

Mocha Pots de Crème

SERVES SIX

This is one of my favorite chocolate desserts, and one of the richest puddings you'll ever have. Children love it, but you might prefer to do as I do and omit the coffee for theirs!

6 ounces/180 g bittersweet (plain) chocolate
1 tablespoon instant coffee granules
3 cups/750 mL/24 fl oz half-and-half (half milk, half cream)
5 egg yolks
½ cup/120 g/4 ounces sugar
3 tablespoons whipped cream, for garnish
6 whole coffee beans, for garnish

In a large saucepan over medium heat, melt the chocolate. Add the coffee and stir until dissolved.

In another small saucepan over medium temperature, heat the half-and-half just to a boil. Set aside.

Place the egg yolks and sugar in a medium stainless steel bowl. Place the bowl over a pot of barely simmering water. Whisk the egg mixture until the sugar is dissolved, or until the mixture is lukewarm (about 98° F/49° C).

Whisk the chocolate mixture into the egg mixture until thoroughly blended. Add ½ cup/ 120 mL/4 fl oz of the hot half-and-half, whisking. Pour the chocolate and egg mixture into the remaining half-and-half in the saucepan. Cook over medium heat for about 5 minutes, or until the mixture thickens or coats the back of a spoon. Pour into 6 coffee or custard cups (about 8 fl oz/250 mL). Chill for at least 4 hours.

Serve topped with whipped cream and whole coffee beans.

Pumpkin Crème Brûlée

SERVES SIX

Such a nice change from pumpkin pie for the holidays!

> ¾ cup/180 g/6 ounces pumpkin puree
> 2¼ cups/560 mL/18 fl oz heavy (double) cream
> 1 vanilla bean, split in half
> 7 egg yolks
> 1 cup/250 g/8 ounces sugar
> 1 teaspoon cinnamon
> ½ teaspoon nutmeg
> ½ teaspoon allspice
> 1 tablespoon chopped crystalized ginger

In a heavy saucepan over medium temperature, heat the pumpkin puree, cream, and vanilla bean halves just to a boil and set aside.

Place the egg yolks and half the sugar in a medium stainless steel bowl and place the bowl over a pot of barely simmering water. Whisk constantly until the mixture forms a ribbon when you lift the whisk, about 6 to 8 minutes. Do not scramble the egg mixture.

Slowly add the hot pumpkin mixture to the egg mixture and, stirring frequently, cook over medium heat until the mixture has the consistency of softly whipped cream, 40 to 50 minutes. Add the cinnamon, nutmeg, allspice, and ginger and mix well. Pour into 6 custard cups (8 fl oz/250 mL) and refrigerate for 3 hours or overnight.

Sprinkle each cream with the remaining sugar and place under a high broiler (grill) for 2 or 3 minutes, or until the sugar is browned. (In my restaurant kitchen, I use a propane torch for this step.)

Serve the Pumpkin Crème Brûlée immediately.

CHAMPAGNE FRUIT COMPOTE

SERVES FOUR

A cup of Champagne Fruit Compote is a very nice way to start breakfast or brunch on a summer's morning as well as to bring a substantial meal to a light and elegant conclusion.

> 2 cups/180 g/6 ounces fresh berries (such as blackberries, strawberries, raspberries, 1 pint)
> 2 cups/180 g/6 ounces ripe melon (such as honeydew or cantaloupe/rock melon)
> ½ cup/120 mL/4 fl oz water
> ¼ cup/60 g/2 ounces sugar
> 1 tablespoon chopped fresh mint
> zest of 1 lemon
> 2 cups/500 mL/16 fl oz Champagne or good-quality sparkling wine, chilled
> sprigs of mint, for garnish
> slices of lemon, for garnish

Rinse and drain the berries. Cut any large ones in half and place in a large bowl. Dice the melon, add to the berries, and toss to combine. Set aside in the refrigerator.

In a small saucepan over high heat, boil the water and sugar to a syrup, about 5 minutes. Add the chopped mint and lemon zest. Remove from the heat and cool to room temperature.

Pour over the mixed fruits and stir gently. Refrigerate for about 30 minutes.

Divide the fruits among 4 wine goblets. Pour the Champagne equally over all. Garnish each serving with a sprig of mint and a slice of lemon. Serve straight away while still cold.

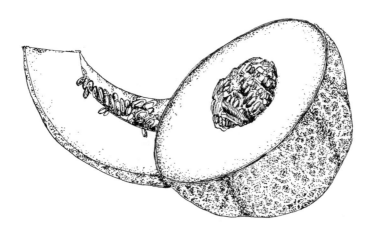

COFFEE GRANITA
SERVES FOUR

This is such a refreshing end to a meal but, believe me, you can eat it any time of day! If you're serving after dinner, though, you might want to use decaffeinated coffee. Use a little sweetened nonfat yogurt instead of the cream and you have an almost guilt-free dessert.

2 cups/500 mL/16 fl oz good-quality brewed coffee
¾ cup/185 g/6 ounces sugar
1 teaspoon ground cinnamon
½ teaspoon ground allspice
¼ teaspoon ground ginger
¼ teaspoon ground cloves

In a medium bowl, mix together the coffee, sugar, cinnamon, allspice, ginger, and cloves and place in the freezer. Stir the mixture about every half hour until frozen, about 6 hours in all, depending on your freezer.

Spoon the Coffee Granita into 4 wine glasses and serve with softly whipped cream and Chocolate Pecan Shortbread (see page 136).

RASPBERRY PORT ICE CREAM

SERVES SIX

There's just nothing like homemade ice cream. It's so rich and custardy. Cooking the raspberries in port makes this another grown-up variation on a nostalgic taste from your childhood.

    2 cups/120 g/4 ounces red raspberries (1 pint)
    6 egg yolks
    1 cup/250 g/8 ounces sugar
    4 cups/1 L/1 quart half-and-half (half milk, half cream)
    1 cup/250 mL/8 fl oz good-quality port

Wash and drain the raspberries. Set aside.

In a small bowl, mix together the egg yolks and half the sugar and set aside.

In a large saucepan over medium temperature, heat the half-and-half and the remaining sugar. Just before the mixture reaches a boil, slowly pour ½ cup/120 mL/4 fl oz of the sweetened half-and-half into the egg mixture in the bowl, whisking constantly. Then pour this mixture back into the saucepan with the remaining half-and-half. Cook until the mixture coats the back of a spoon, about 5 minutes. Cool this ice-cream base on the countertop for about 15 minutes then set aside in the refrigerator to chill completely.

Meanwhile, in another saucepan cook the raspberries and port over high heat until they reach the consistency of jam, about 5 minutes. Set aside in the refrigerator to chill.

Mix the chilled raspberries and ice-cream base together well. Freeze in your ice-cream maker according to the manufacturer's instructions.

CAPRIAL'S JAMMERS

MAKES ONE DOZEN COOKIES

These cookies are so much fun to make with children: they love to smash them flat and stick their thumbs in them. They love to eat them, too! Feel free to use whatever flavor jam you (or they) care for.

2 cups/315 g/10 ounces all-purpose (plain) flour
¾ cup/145 g/4 ounces confectioners' (icing) sugar
1 egg
1 cup/250 g/8 ounces unsalted butter
1 teaspoon vanilla extract
1 teaspoon salt
⅓ cup/80 mL/3 fl oz raspberry jam

Preheat the oven to 350° F/175° C/gas mark 4.

In a food processor, place the flour, sugar, and egg. Turn the machine on and slowly add the butter, 2 tablespoons/30 g/1 ounce at a time. Add the vanilla and salt. Process until the dough forms a ball on top of the blades.

With the palms of your hands, roll the dough into balls about 2 inches/5 cm diameter. Place the balls on a greased baking sheet. Press the balls down slightly with the bottom of a glass or jar to a thickness of ¼ inch/0.5 cm. Press your thumb into the middle of each circle to form a well, without pressing all the way through the dough.

Fill each well with about ½ teaspoon of the jam. Bake until the cookies are golden brown, about 10 to 12 minutes.

Serve alone or with Raspberry Port Ice Cream (see the previous page).

CHOCOLATE PECAN SHORTBREAD
MAKES EIGHTEEN COOKIES

These are my favorite cookies. I came up with the recipe when my sister, who can't eat eggs, asked for (begged for) a chocolate cookie without eggs. Flattening the cookies turns them nice and crispy and you can make them even crunchier by topping them with crystalized sugar rather than the granulated.

1½ cups/250 g/8 ounces all-purpose (plain) flour
½ cup/90 g/3 ounces unsweetened cocoa powder
½ cup/90 g/3 ounces confectioners' (icing) sugar
1 cup/250 g/8 ounces unsalted butter
½ teaspoon vanilla extract
1 cup/250 g/8 ounces granulated sugar
½ cup/60 g/2 ounces ground pecans

Preheat the oven to 350° F/175° C/gas mark 4. Grease a baking sheet well.

Place the flour, cocoa, and confectioners' sugar in a food processor. Turn the machine on and slowly add the butter, 2 tablespoons/30 g/1 ounce at a time. Add the vanilla and process until the dough forms a ball on top of the blades.

In the palms of your hands, roll the dough into circles about ½ inch/1 cm thick. Place on the prepared baking sheet and press each circle of dough down with the bottom of a glass until it is about ¼ inch/0.5 cm thick. Sprinkle the dough with the granulated sugar and pecans and press again to flatten. Bake the cookies until brown, about 10 minutes. Cool them on the baking sheet before serving.

opposite: Chocolate Pecan Shortbread, this page; and on the page following: Caprial with her husband, John; and, below, Kurt Spak, night chef at the restaurant, and Mark Dowers, the day chef.

BASICS

- Beef, Veal, or Lamb Stock   *139*
- Fish Stock   *140*
- Chicken Stock   *141*
- Vegetable Stock   *141*
- Salsa   *142*
- Basic Cream Sauce   *142*
- Crème Fraîche   *143*
- Mayonnaise   *143*
- Roasted Garlic   *144*
- Roasted Shallots   *144*
- Roasted Peppers   *144*
- Honey Wheat Bread   *145*
- Pound Cake   *146*
- Berry Orange Sauce   *146*

Beef, Veal, or Lamb Stock
MAKES ABOUT 4 CUPS / 1 L / 32 FL OZ

Every chef will tell you there's nothing like a good homemade stock, using the freshest ingredients. And it's true. Here are my recipes for meat, chicken, fish, and vegetables. They're indispensable, so I suggest keeping batches of them in the freezer.

> 5 pounds/2.5 kg beef, veal, or lamb bones
> 2 onions, roughly chopped
> 1 carrot, roughly chopped
> 3 stalks celery, roughly chopped
> 3 cloves garlic, chopped
> 2 tablespoons tomato paste (puree)
> 1 cup/250 mL/8 fl oz dry red wine
> 8 cups/2 L/64 fl oz water
> 1 bay leaf

Preheat the oven to 450° F/225° C/gas mark 8.

In a roasting pan, place the bones, onions, carrot, celery, and garlic and roast for about 1 hour, or until the bones turn golden brown. Spread the tomato paste over the mixture and roast for 10 more minutes.

Transfer the mixture to a large stockpot. Add the wine to the roasting pan and, using a wooden spoon, scrape up all the brown bits from the bottom of the pan. Pour this liquid into the stockpot. Add the water and bay leaf. Bring to a boil over high heat. Reduce the heat and simmer for 6 to 8 hours, until the stock is full of flavor. Strain through a fine sieve into a bowl and use immediately, or allow to cool to room temperature before refrigerating.

This stock keeps in the refrigerator for up to one week and can be frozen.

FISH STOCK

MAKES ABOUT 4 CUPS / 1 L / 32 FL OZ

½ pounds/750 g fish bones (use bones from white fish only)
2 leeks
1 tablespoon/15 g/½ ounce unsalted butter
2 large onions, roughly chopped
2 stalks celery, roughly chopped
3 cloves garlic, chopped
¼ cup/30 g/1 ounce mushroom stems
1 cup/120 mL/8 fl oz dry white wine
4 sprigs thyme
8 cups/2 L/64 fl oz water

Roughly chop the fish bones and place them in a large bowl or stockpot. Cover with cold water and soak for 1 or 2 hours to remove any remaining traces of blood.

Discard the green portion of the leeks. Trim and rinse the whites thoroughly, then roughly chop. In a large stockpot over high temperature, heat the butter until bubbling. Add the leeks, onions, celery, garlic, and mushroom stems and sauté until they begin to give off their aroma, 3 or 4 minutes. Add the wine and bones, reduce heat, and sweat the mixture, covered, for about 8 minutes. Add the thyme and water and simmer, uncovered, for 25 minutes more. Strain through a fine sieve into a bowl and use immediately, or allow to cool to room temperature before refrigerating.

This stock keeps in the refrigerator for up to one week and can be frozen.

CHICKEN STOCK

MAKES ABOUT 4 CUPS / 1 L / 32 FL OZ

2 pounds/1 kg chicken bones, rinsed
2 onions, roughly chopped
2 carrots, roughly chopped
3 stalks celery, roughly chopped
3 cloves garlic, chopped
4 sprigs thyme
8 cups/2 L/64 fl oz water
1 bay leaf

In a large stockpot over high heat, bring the bones, onions, carrots, celery, garlic, thyme, and water just to a boil. Add the bay leaf. Reduce the heat and simmer for 4 to 6 hours, or until the stock is richly flavored. Strain through a fine sieve into a bowl and use immediately, or allow to cool to room temperature before refrigerating.

This stock keeps in the refrigerator for up to one week and can be frozen.

■ ■ ■

VEGETABLE STOCK

MAKES ABOUT 4 CUPS / 1 L / 32 FL OZ

3 onions, roughly chopped
4 carrots, roughly chopped
5 stalks celery, roughly chopped
4 ounces/120 g mushrooms, roughly chopped
4 cloves garlic, chopped
3 shallots, chopped
6 sprigs thyme
8 cups/2 L/64 fl oz water

In a large stockpot over high heat, bring the onions, carrots, celery, mushrooms, garlic, shallots, thyme, and water just to a boil. Reduce the heat and simmer for about 1 hour, until the stock has a rich full flavor. Strain through a fine sieve into a bowl and use immediately, or allow to cool to room temperature before refrigerating.

This stock keeps in the refrigerator for up to one week and can be frozen.

SALSA

MAKES ABOUT 1 CUP / 120 ML / 8 FL OZ

Here's a basic salsa recipe for you to serve with tortilla chips or as an accompaniment to meat, fish, or poultry. Spice it up, spice it down, as you wish, and feel free to experiment with different peppers.

    3 tomatoes, seded and diced
    1 small red (Spanish) onion, minced
    2 cloves garlic, minced
    2 jalapeño peppers, seeded and chopped
    ¼ cup/60 mL/2 fl oz cayenne or chile sauce
    1 teaspoon ground cumin
    ½ teaspoon ground coriander
    ½ teaspoon chile powder
    salt and freshly ground black pepper, to taste

Place all the ingredients in a nonreactive bowl and mix well. Set aside for at least 30 minutes to allow the flavors to meld and develop.

■ ■ ■

BASIC CREAM SAUCE

MAKES ABOUT 1 CUP / 120 ML / 8 FL OZ

It's good to have one standard cream sauce at your fingertips to dress up simple entrees or to serve with pasta. You can add just about anything to this one—herbs, cheese, sundried tomatoes. Use your imagination!

    2 cloves garlic, chopped
    2 shallots, chopped
    1 cup/120 mL/8 fl oz dry white wine
    1½ cups/180 mL/12 fl oz heavy (double) cream
    salt and white pepper, to taste

In a medium saucepan over high heat, cook the garlic, shallots, and wine until half the liquid has evaporated, 3 to 5 minutes. Add the cream and cook until the liquid has reduced by half again and is thick enough to coat the back of a spoon, 4 to 6 minutes. Season with salt and pepper.

Use immediately, or allow to cool, then refrigerate for up to 10 days.

CRÈME FRAÎCHE

MAKES ABOUT 2 CUPS / 500 ML / 16 FL OZ

Although you can use crème fraîche just as you would sour cream, it's richer—and *so* much better.

    2 cups/500 mL/16 fl oz heavy (double) cream
    2 heaping tablespoons sour cream

In a glass bowl, whisk together the cream and sour cream. Cover with cheesecloth and set aside on the countertop overnight.

    Refrigerate for 4 hours before using or for up to 2 weeks.

■ ■ ■

MAYONNAISE

MAKES ABOUT 2 CUPS / 500 ML / 16 FL OZ

Here's another recipe that you can serve just as is or transform with your imagination. Finely chopped herbs, roasted peppers, even some unexpected dried cherries are all delicious.

    ¼ cup/60 mL/2 fl oz white wine vinegar
    2 tablespoons Dijon mustard
    2 shallots, minced
    2 cloves garlic, minced
    2 large egg yolks
    1⅓ cups/340 mL/11 fl oz vegetable oil
    1 teaspoon fresh lemon juice
    salt and freshly ground white pepper, to taste

In a food processor, blend the vinegar, mustard, shallots, garlic, and egg yolks together well. With the motor running, gradually drizzle in half the vegetable oil. Scrape down the sides of the bowl. Turn the processor back on and continue to add in the remaining oil in a slow, steady stream until thoroughly blended and the mixture is smooth and thick. Add the lemon juice, season with salt and pepper, and mix well.

    Use immediately or refrigerate for up to 2 weeks.

ROASTED GARLIC

For a tasty appetizer, spread this garlic on bread and serve with mustard and goat cheese.

> 1 head garlic
> 2 tablespoons olive oil

Preheat the oven to 250° F/125° C/gas mark ½.

Slice about ¼ inch/7 mm off the top of the garlic head and discard. Place the head in a small baking dish or ovenproof sauté pan. Drizzle over the oil. Roast until soft, 40 to 50 minutes.

Roasted Garlic will keep in the refrigerator for 2 or 3 weeks.

■ ■ ■

ROASTED SHALLOTS

Roasted shallots are also wonderful with steaks and grilled chicken.

> 6 shallots, peeled
> ¼ cup/60 mL/2 fl oz olive oil

Preheat the oven to 250° F/125° C/gas mark ½.

Place the shallots and olive oil in a small baking dish or ovenproof sauté pan and roast until soft, about 40 minutes.

Roasted Shallots will keep in the refrigerator for up to 2 weeks.

■ ■ ■

ROASTED PEPPERS

Once you start roasting peppers, you won't be able to stop. Add them to pastas, soups, salads. Bell peppers are also good just by themselves!

> red bell peppers (capsicums), jalapeño or other peppers

Preheat the broiler (grill). Place the peppers on a baking sheet or in a shallow ovenproof dish and broil (grill) until the skins blister and turn brown. Turn the peppers until charred on all sides, about 15 minutes. Transfer the roasted peppers to a bowl, cover with plastic wrap (plastic film), and set aside to cool.

When the peppers are cool enough to handle, peel the skins and remove stems and seeds.

Use immediately or drizzle with olive oil and store in the refrigerator for up to 2 months.

HONEY WHEAT BREAD

MAKES TWO 2-POUND / 1-KG LOAVES

This is the bread we use most at the restaurant, it's so versatile. We particularly like it for the Eggplant Sandwich.

    3 cups/750 mL/24 fl oz water, heated to 110° F/55° C
    4 tablespoons active dry yeast
    ½ cup/120 mL/4 fl oz (clear) honey
    1 cup/155 g/5 ounces oat bran
    1 cup/155 g/5 ounces wheat bran
    2 cups/500 mL/16 fl oz milk, heated to 150° F/75° C
    4 cups/620 g/20 ounces whole wheat (wholemeal) flour
    6 to 7 cups/930 g to 1.1 kg/30 to 35 ounces bread flour
    2 tablespoons salt
    2 teaspoons olive oil

In an electric mixer, using the dough hook, mix together the water, yeast, and honey. Set aside for 10 minutes until the yeast is foamy.

Add the oat and wheat brans to the yeast mixture and blend together. Add the milk and mix again.

With the motor running, slowly add the whole wheat flour, then 6 cups/930 g/30 ounces of the bread flour. If the mixture seems too moist, add a little more flour. When the flour is fully incorporated, add the salt. Run the machine for another 2 to 3 minutes until a smooth, soft dough is formed.

Oil a very large bowl with the olive oil. Place the dough in the bowl and then flip it over to coat the other side. Cover the bowl with a towel and place it in a warm spot. Let the dough rise until it has doubled in bulk, about 1 hour.

Twenty minutes before the dough has finished rising, preheat the oven to 400° F/200° C/ gas mark 6.

Punch the dough down with your fist and divide it in half. Form the dough into 2 loaves and place them in well-greased loaf pans. Bake for 50 minutes to 1 hour, or until the bread has a hollow sound when the bottom of the loaf pan is tapped. Remove the loaves from the pans and place them on a rack. Set the loaves aside to cool well before slicing, at least 20 minutes.

POUND CAKE

MAKES ONE CAKE

Pound cake is always good, but it's especially good with a dollop of Crème Fraîche and some fresh berries or a scoop of ice cream and Berry Orange Sauce.

> 1 cup/250 g/8 ounces unsalted butter
> 2 cups/500 g/16 ounces sugar
> ¼ cup/80 mL/2½ ounces almond paste
> 4 whole eggs
> 1 egg yolk
> 2 cups/310 g/10 ounces all-purpose (plain) flour
> ½ teaspoon vanilla extract
> ½ teaspoon almond extract
> zest of 1 lemon

Preheat the oven to 350° F/175° C/gas mark 4. Grease a bundt or ring pan well.

Place the butter, sugar, and almond paste in the bowl of an electric mixer. Using the paddle attachment, beat on medium speed until smooth. Add the eggs and the yolk one at a time, blending each in fully before incorporating the next. Mix in the flour just until the batter comes together. Add the vanilla and almond extracts and zest and mix just until blended.

Pour the batter into the prepared pan and bake for 40 minutes to 1 hour, until a tester inserted in the center comes out clean. After 10 minutes, invert onto a rack to cool.

■ ■ ■

BERRY ORANGE SAUCE

MAKES ABOUT 1 CUP / 120 ML / 8 FL OZ

You can use both blackberries and/or raspberries in this sauce. It's handy for using up overripe berries and for keeping in the freezer for a quick dessert sauce.

> 3 cups/270 g/8 ounces raspberries or blackberries (1½ pints)
> ½ cup/125 g/4 ounces sugar
> 1 teaspoon orange juice concentrate
> ½ teaspoon orange zest

In a medium saucepan over high heat, cook the berries and sugar until the sugar melts. Continue cooking until about half the resulting liquid evaporates and the mixture is thick and syrupy, 5 or 6 minutes. Stir in the orange juice concentrate. Strain through a fine sieve and discard the seeds. Return the sauce to the pan and add the zest. Cook over medium heat for 3 or 4 minutes to bring out the flavor of the zest.

Use warm or chilled. Keeps in the refrigerator for up to 2 weeks.

GLOSSARY

Butterfly	To cut a piece of beef, poultry, etc., nearly all the way through and open it out to make it twice as long but half as thick as it was. The meat should then be evened out using a meat mallet.
Caramelize	With sugar, to cook over heat until brown to enrich the flavor. With meat and vegetables, to cook over high heat to bring out and brown the natural sugars, adding an intensity of flavor.
Deglaze	To add liquid to a cooking pan and stir with a wooden spoon to mix in all the brown bits stuck to the bottom.
Diced	Cut into ⅓-inch (1-cm) cubes. Finely diced is cut into ¼-inch (7-mm) cubes; diced large is cut into ¾-inch (2-cm) cubes.
Emulsify	To completely blend together an oil or fat with an acid such as vinegar or lemon juice.
Julienned	Cut into matchsticks about ⅛ inch (3 mm) across by 2 inches (5 cm) long.
Nonreactive bowl	A glass, ceramic, or stainless steel bowl, not an aluminum or cast-iron one. It's important to use only nonreactive containers when preparing and storing dishes, such as dressings or marinades, which contain acidic ingredients such as vinegar or lemon juice.
Reduce	To thicken and intensify the flavor of a sauce by boiling it down through evaporation.
Sweat	To cover an ingredient with liquid and barely simmer it to bring out the flavors.

INDEX

Italics refer to cross references for menu suggestions.

Aïoli
    green peppercorn, 79
    red pepper, 66
    smoked onion, 3
Almond crust, 113
Apple
    Almond Bread Pudding, *78*, 126
    Brandy Stuffing, 88
    Curry Sauce, 72
    Tart, 115
Artichokes, grilled, 109
Arugula. *Same as* rocket
Arugula pesto, 81
Asian Barbecue Sauce, 82
Asian Cole Slaw, 53
Asian Vegetable Soup, 27
Asparagus, lemon pepper, 108
Aubergine. *See* Eggplant

■

Bacon Thyme Dressing, 47
Basic Cream Sauce, 142
Bean
    salad, 52
    soup, 31
    spread, 9
Beef
    flank steak with aïoli, 79
    flank steak with barbecue, 82
    ossobuco, 78
    salad, 83
    Stock, 139
    Stew, 77
    tenderloin with hollandaise, 80
    tenderloin with Pesto, 81
Bell Pepper. *Same as* capsicum
    Aïoli, 66
    & Olive Puree, 71
    & Olive Tapinade, 36
    roasted, 144
    Vinaigrette, 51
Berry Orange Sauce, *114*, 146
Berry Trifles, 127
Black Pepper Dressing, 83

Blackberry Lemon Soufflés, 125
Bread pudding, apple almond, 126
Bread salad, 51
Broccoli, marinated, 110
Brûlée
    orange crème, 128
    pumpkin crème, 131
Bruschetta, tomato, 7

■

Cabbage salad, 17
Cake
    crab, 66
    peach upside-down, 124
    plum spice, 121
    pound, 146
Caprial's Jammers, 135
Champagne Fruit Compote, *87, 94,* 132
Cheese
    garlic goat, 5
    Puffs, 11
    Quesadillas, 10
Cheesecake
    chocolate almond, 122
    white chocolate, 123
Chicken
    game hens, 73
    grilled with olive puree, 71
    sautéed, 72
    stuffed, 75
    Liver Pâté, 13
    Salad Sandwich, 38
    Stock, 141
    stuffed with apples, 75
Chipotle pepper gazpacho, 30
Chocolate
    Almond Cheesecake, *5, 68,* 122
    Crust, 113
    Hazelnut Torte, 120
    Pecan Shortbread, *133*, 136
    Praline Tart, *72*, 116
Cilantro. *Same as* coriander
Cinnamon Rum Flan, 10, 89, 129
Coffee Granita, 80, 133

Cole slaw, Asian, 53
Compote, fruit, 132
Cookies, jam, 135
Coriander. *Same as* cilantro
Courgette. *Same as* zucchini
Couscous Salad, *54*, 79
Crab Cakes, 66
Cream, garlic, 92
    sauce, 142
Crème Fraîche, 26, 31, 44, 124, 143
Croutons, 83
Crust
    almond, 113
    chocolate, 116
    cinnamon, 117
    garlic, 8
    shortening, 115
    sweet, 114
    toasted almond, 122
Custard, herb, 15

■

Dressing
    bacon thyme, 47
    black pepper, 83
    ginger & cherry, 49
    orange ginger, 45
    sage walnut, 48
    shallot, 91
    tomato & horseradish, 44
Duckling, roasted, 76

■

Eggplant
    marinated, 36
    relish, 63
    Sandwich, 36, *145*
    tapenade, 16

■

Fettucine & Mushrooms, 94
Filling
    apple tart, 115
    cheesecake, 122
    peach tart, 113, 117
    praline tart, 116
    raspberry lemon tart, 114
    spinach, 8

Fish, *see also* individual types
    pan-fried with nuts, 69
    sauce, 27
    stock, 140
Flan, cinnamon rum, 129
Fried Fish with Nut Crust, 69
Fried potatoes, 105

■

Game Hen, roasted, *10*, 73
Garlic
    Cream, 92
    roasted, 144
    & Tomato Soup, 6
Gazpacho, 30
Ginger
    & Basil Butter Sauce, 65
    & Cherry Dressing, 49
    Peach Upside-Down Cake, 124
Greens. *See also* Spinach, Cole Slaw,
Radicchio
    and lime vinaigrette, 62
    pepper vinaigrette, 51
    sautèed, 91

■

Halibut
    baked with salsa, 61
    poached in saffron, 68
Hazelnut & Gorgonzola Cream Sauce, 87
Herb
    Custards, 15
    roasted, 103
Herbed Oven-Roasted Fries, 86
Hollandaise, peppercorn, 80
Honey Wheat Bread, *23*, *36*, 145

■

Ice cream, raspberry, 134

■

Jammers, 88
John's Sesame Noodles, *90*, 101

■

Lamb
    Burgers, 86
    leg with hazelnut sauce, 87

shanks with mushrooms, 84
Stew, 85
stock, 139
Leek Soup, 23
Lemon Sauce, 125
Lentil & Pepper Soup, 25
Lime Vinaigrette, 46

■

Marinade, Citrus, 62
Mayonnaise, *37-38*, 143
Mocha Pots de Crème, *31*, *73*, 130
Mushroom sauce, 84
Mushrooms, cheese stuffed, 5
Mussels
    Soup, 29
    Steamed, 14
    Stew, 67

■

New York Salad, 83
Noodles, John's Sesame, 101

■

Olive & Eggplant Tapenade, 16
Onion
    Aïoli, 3
    smoking, 3
Orange Crème Brûlée, *91*, 128
Orange Ginger Dressing, 45
Ossobuco, 78
Oysters
    baked, 4
    pan-fried with salad, 17
    sautéed with relish, 6

■

Pancake, potato, 106
Pancetta, 92
Papaya Salsa, 61
Pasta
    couscous salad, 54
    fettucine with mushrooms, 94
    penne with garlic, 92
    ziti with cheeses, 93
Pâté, chicken liver, 13
Pea Soup, 26, *70*
Peach Upside-Down Cake, 62

Pears
    Tart, 117
    and scallops, 60
Penne, 92
Peppercorn Hollandaise, 80
Peppers. See also Bell Peppers
    Gazpacho, 30
    roasted, 144
Pesto, 96
    arugula, 81
Pizza, pesto, 96
Plum
    Puree, 90
    Spice Cake, *14*, 121
Poached Pear Tart, *84*, *95*, 117
Polenta, 77
    grilled, 18
    with Roasted Herbs, 103
Pork
    chops, roasted and stuffed, 89
    roasted, with greens, 91
    with stuffing, 88
    sandwich, 39
    tenderloin with plums, 90
Potatoes
    gratin, *15*, 104
    mashed, 85
    oven-roasted fries, 105
    Pancake, 106
    salad, 55
Potstickers, vegetable, 12
Pound Cake, *127*, 146
Poussins, 73
Praline Tart, 116
Prawns
    glazed, 64
    sautéed with peppers, 19
Pumpkin Crème Brûlée, *74*, 131
Puree
    pepper & olive, 71
    plum, 90

■

Quesadillas, cheese, 10

■

Radicchio Salad, 50, 75
Ragoût, vegetable, 59

Raspberry
    Lemon Curd Tart, *69*, 144
    Port Ice Cream, *3*, *88*, 134, *135*
    Ricotta Tart, *15*, *64*, 118
Relish
    eggplant, 63
    shallot, 39
    tomato pepper, 6
Rice
    fried with shiitake, 76
    Pilaf, 102
Ricotta Raspberry Tart, *15*, *64*, 118
Roast Duckling & Fried Rice, 12
Roast Pork with Sautéed Greens, 24
Roasted Bell Peppers, 144
Roasted Garlic, 144
Roasted Pepper & Lentil Soup, 18
Roasted Shallots, 144
Roasted Vegetables, 87
Rocket. *Same as* arugula
Rosemary & Dried Cherry Stuffing, 89

Sage & Walnut Dressing, 48
Salad
    cabbage, 17
    couscous, 54
    New York, 83
    radicchio, 50
    shrimp, 70
    spinach, 47-49
    steak, 83
    tomato & bean, 52
    yellow fin potato, 55
Salmon
    with ginger and basil sauce, 65
    grilled with citrus marinade, 62
    Sandwich, 37
    steamed with vegetables, 59
Salsa, 142
    corn, 73
    papaya, 61
Sandwich
    chicken salad, 38
    eggplant, 36
    pork tenderloin, 39
    smoked salmon, 37
    vegetable, 35

Sauce
    apple curry, 72
    Asian barbecue, 82
    basic cream, 142
    berry orange, 146
    ginger basil, 65
    hazelnut & gorgonzola cream, 87
    lemon, 125
    mushroom, 84
    roasted tomato, 18
Scallops
    poached with pears, 60
    Soup, 32
Shallots
    Dressing, 91
    Relish, 39
    roasted, 144
Shiitake Fried Rice, 76
Shortbread, chocolate pecan, 136
Shortening Crust, 119
Shrimp
    with aïoli, 3
    salad, 70
Soufflés, blackberry lemon, 125
Soup
    Asian vegetable, 27
    black bean, 31
    gazpacho, 30
    leek, 23
    mussel, 29
    pea, 26
    pepper & lentil, 25
    scallop, 32
    squash, 28
    tomato & garlic, 24
Spinach
    filling, 8
    Salads, 47-49
    Thyme Tart, 8
Spread, white bean, 9
Squash Soup, 28
Steak
    with Barbecue Sauce, *14*, 82
    with Peppercorn Aïoli, 79
    salad, 82
Stew
    beef, 77
    lamb, 85

mussel, 67
Stir-Fry Vegetables, 95
Stock
    beef, 77, 139
    chicken, 9, 12, 23-28, 31, 39, 54, 74, 77-78,
    88-89, 102-3, 141
    fish, 32, 60, 68, 140
    lamb, 84-84, 139
    vegetable, 9, 12, 23, 54, 60, 77, 85, 89, 102-3,
    141
    veal, 78
Strawberry
    Peach Tart, *71*, 113
    Streusel, *85*, 119
Stuffed chicken, 75
Stuffing
    apple brandy, 88
    rosemary & cherry, 89
    walnut & cranberry, 74
Sugar, browning with torch, 128, 131

■

Tapenade
    olive & eggplant, 16
    pepper & olive, 36
Tart
    apple, 115
    chocolate praline, 116
    poached pear, 117
    raspberry lemon, 114
    ricotta raspberry , 118
    spinach thyme, 8
    strawberry peach, 113
Tomato
    Bruscetta, 7
    dressing, *8*, 44

sauce, 18
Soup, & Garlic, 24
    Mussel, 29
Torch, to brown sugar, 128, 131
Torte, chocolate hazelnut, 120
Triple Chocolate Hazelnut Torte, 60
Tuna, 63
Turkey, roasted, 74

■

Veal
    shanks, 78
    stock, 139
Vegetable
    Potstickers, 12
    Ragoût, 59
    roasted, 107
    sandwich, 35
    soup, 27
    stir-fry, 95
    Stock, 141
Vinaigrette
    balsamic, 55
    greens, 46
    lime, 46
    simple, 43
    yellow pepper, 51

■

Walnut & Cranberry Stuffing, 74
White Bean Spread, 9
White Chocolate Cheesecake, *61*, 123

■

Ziti, baked, 93
Zucchini. *Same as* courgette